M000209115

"You won't find a better guide than Edward Sri to take you by the hand and walk you through the Gospel of Matthew. A trained scholar who writes like a popular novelist, Sri explains the Jewish background and Old Testament context that makes Matthew come alive!"

- JOHN BERSGMA
Author of *Bible Basics for Catholics*

"Edward Sri has moved us beyond the typical modern limitations in reading Matthew. Read this book attentively, then, and you'll come to a deeper love of the people and the religion of Israel, the people and the religion of our Messiah and King."

- SCOTT HAHN
Bestselling Author of *The First Society*

"Through this dynamic Bible study, Sri shows us why his courses are overflowing with excited students—he makes the Scriptures come alive."

- CURTIS A. MARTIN
Founder, FOCUS

"Edward Sri has uncovered and clearly presented the Old Testament background needed to flesh out our understanding of Matthew's Gospel. The result is a better understanding of Jesus's life and mission—and ours."

- STACY MITCH
Author of the Courageous Women Bible study series

GOD

WITH

US

GOD
WITH
US

ENCOUNTERING JESUS
IN THE GOSPEL OF
MATTHEW

EDWARD SRI

Foreword by Scott Hahn

EMMAUS
ROAD
PUBLISHING

Emmaus Road Publishing
1468 Parkview Circle
Steubenville, Ohio 43952

Library of Congress Control no: 2019948949
ISBN: 978-1-64585-000-7

Cover design and layout by
Emily Demary

Cover image:
Landscape and water at the Sea of Galilee, Israel.
Photo by Chris Gallimore.

To my father and mother, Prasit and Antoinette Sri, with love and gratitude.

CONTENTS

Foreword

TWENTY YEARS AGO, a soon-to-be degreed Edward Sri approached me with an idea for a Bible study to be published by the newly founded Emmaus Road Publishing. What could I say? Dr. Sri was one of my best students, and I knew that the approach he would take to unpack the Gospel of Matthew was one I myself found invaluable.

I knew that Sri would carry the banner of St. Augustine, applying to his study of Matthew the notion that the New Testament is concealed in the Old, and the Old is revealed in the New. He has done so in a magnetically powerful way, using the principle of typology to underscore one of Matthew's strongest and most consistent themes: the kingdom of heaven, whose King is Jesus.

What I didn't know twenty years ago was that this study on Matthew's Gospel would do so much more than break down the pages of Scripture. Far from being just a resource for those with an academic interest in Scripture, Sri's study, originally titled *Mystery of the Kingdom*, has proven to be a source of spiritual nourishment.

Sri has put his many years of experience to the service of expanding and improving what was already an exceptional text. The revised study you hold in your hands, *God with Us: Encountering Jesus in the Gospel of Matthew*, reflects Sri's desire to highlight Jesus' identity as our Messiah King, *Emmanuel*—truly God with us. In it, Sri helps us to understand who Jesus is first by understanding Jesus' kingdom.

The apostate scholar Alfred Loisy criticized Jesus for promising the kingdom, when all he left us was the Church. But what Jesus promised and what he delivered are one and the same. In the words of the Second Vatican Council:

> To carry out the will of the Father Christ inaugurated the kingdom of heaven on earth and revealed to us his mystery; by his obedience he brought about our redemption. The Church—that is, the kingdom of Christ already present in mystery—grows visibly through the power of God in the world. (*Lumen Gentium*, no. 3)

The kingdom is where the King is present.

God with Us remains as relevant for study as it is enriching for personal prayer. I thank my student, Dr. Sri, who has now become a beloved teacher to so many searching for a savior just as eagerly as the first-century Jews. May this book move you to a deeper love of Jesus and his kingdom.

Scott Hahn
Steubenville, Ohio

Introduction

God with Us

MUCH HAS BEEN SAID about why Jesus died. This book, however, will focus on why Jesus lived.

While the death and Resurrection are the most crucial chapters in the story of Jesus, he did a lot more with his life than offer it up on the Cross. In fact, we won't fully appreciate the significance of his death on Good Friday until we understand the mission that Jesus had for his life in the years that went before.

What was that mission? First, we know that Jesus became a famous teacher who quickly won the hearts and respect of many Jewish people. We also know that Jesus was renowned for his powerful actions of curing the sick, raising the dead, giving sight to the blind, and expelling evil spirits. With his popularity rapidly skyrocketing, large crowds began to follow him from town to town. Some people gave up everything to become his disciples. Others went so far as to claim him as their

1

king, pinning their hopes on him as the one who would bring Israel's history to its ultimate destination and its moment of glory.

At the same time, Jesus was also known for being somewhat of a troublemaker. His teachings stirred up great controversy, and he met with fierce opposition from the religious leaders of his day. Many of his public actions were considered out of line with traditional Jewish piety. Even his private social life was under intense scrutiny: in the eyes of some, Jesus was hanging out with all the wrong people—the sinners, lepers, drunkards, and other outcasts with whom most pious Jews would not want to be closely associated.

Moreover, Jesus frequently challenged the ideologies and practices of many Jewish leaders, exposing their hypocrisy and subverting their very authority. He even went after Israel's most sacred symbol, the Temple, as he stormed into this holiest of buildings and turned the place upside down, flipping over tables and predicting the Temple's imminent destruction. Actions such as these weren't the best way to "win friends and influence people" in first-century Judaism. In fact, they brought on many enemies and ultimately cost him his life.

Most of all, Jesus said and did things that the ancient Jews believed only God can do. He calmed the storms and the sea, which was something only the creator could do (Pss. 18:15; 104;7; 107:28–29; Mt. 8:26–27). He forgave sins by his own authority, which was something only God could do (Mt. 9:1–3). He also taught with his own authority in a shocking way that put himself on par with God. He quoted some of the

Ten Commandments given by God on Mount Sinai and then said, "But I say to you," as he introduced an expansion or deepening of the divine law given to Moses. Think about how alarming that would have been to the ancient Jews hearing this: Who does this Jesus think he is? How can he quote God and then say, "But *I* say to you"? Who is Jesus to add on to, expand, or deepen what God himself gave us in the Ten Commandments?

Matthew would answer these questions with the unique title he gives to Jesus in the opening chapter of his Gospel. For Matthew, Jesus is not just a leader of a counter-cultural movement. He's not just a teacher, miracle worker, or prophet sent from God. He's not just Israel's savior or redeemer. Jesus is Emmanuel, which means God with us (1:23).

So when we look upon Jesus in Matthew's Gospel, we must remember we are encountering the face of God. Indeed, the story in Matthew's Gospel is the story of the God who is with us in his Son, Jesus Christ. At the start of the Gospel, Jesus is introduced as "Emmanuel." And the kingdom that Jesus is establishing throughout the Gospel of Matthew is all about bringing people back into union with God—not just the faithful Jews of his day but also the sinners, the outcasts, the suffering, and even the gentiles, the non-Jewish people from all the other nations. God will be with his people again through Christ's kingdom that is breaking down the barriers, going out to the peripheries, calling people to repentance, and reconciling all humanity to the Father.

It's not surprising, therefore, that we'll see this theme again at the very close of Matthew's Gospel.

After his death and Resurrection, Jesus commissions the apostles to go make disciples of all nations and he promises, "*I am with you always*, even to the close of the age" (Mt. 28:20). So from beginning to end, the theme of Emmanuel—the theme of God with us—radiates through Matthew's Gospel in the kingdom Jesus is building.

But if we want to understand how God is with us through Christ's kingdom, there's one other title we must grasp: Jesus is the messiah, the king.

Jesus' life is like a mosaic—a collection of small pieces of colored stones or tile cemented on a flat surface in such a way that, when all the pieces are viewed together, they form a larger picture. However, if each colored stone is looked at individually, isolated from the other stones, the larger image will be missed. To gaze upon a mosaic, one must step back and look at the picture as a whole in order to see how all the pieces fit together to form one beautiful work of art.

He's not just a teacher, miracle worker or prophet. Jesus is Emmanuel...God with us.

In a similar way, we might be familiar with various pieces of Jesus' ministry—his walking on water, healing a leper, giving the Sermon on the Mount, teaching the parable of the sower, giving Peter the "keys of the kingdom," and riding into Jerusalem on a donkey. But do we understand how every little detail of his life, every word and every action, fits together in his one overarching mission to build his kingdom? If we only look at the isolated little parts—the smaller stories of Christ's life—we will miss the larger picture and not understand his saving mission and the Church he founded. This book is meant to help us step back and look at how all his words and actions actually fit together into one larger plan. At the center of that plan is Jesus' mission to build the kingdom of heaven on earth.

As we'll see, Jesus considered himself to be Israel's long-awaited king—the prophesied "anointed one," or "messiah"—who would bring God's plan for Israel to fulfillment and empower Israel to be what it was always meant to be. This mission of building his kingdom was at the center of his teachings and at the heart of all his actions. So whether we're considering his great sermons, parables, and confrontations with the Pharisees, or we're reading about his baptism at the Jordan, temptations in the desert, and healing the sick, we need to see that all the little pieces of Jesus' life are strategic parts of his kingdom-building plan. And once we see how the small pieces fit together in the larger whole, we will more greatly appreciate the beautiful masterpiece that God has accomplished in his death and Resurrection.

METICULOUS MATTHEW

This book will assist the reader in a study of Christ's life and mission as seen through the lens of Saint Matthew's Gospel. Pope St. John Paul II once called Matthew "the catechist's Gospel"—perhaps because Matthew is arguably the most highly structured Gospel, making it easy to use for teaching. It's also the Gospel that most clearly makes connections between the Old Testament and Jesus, meticulously highlighting every step of the way how Old Testament prophecies, hopes, and expectations are brought to fulfillment in practically every detail of Christ's life.

More than the other Gospels, Matthew brings together most explicitly this central theme of Jesus' mission, the building of the kingdom. This, of course, has tremendous value not only for understanding Jesus' life, but also for seeing how Jesus continues to carry out his mission today through his Church. Indeed, Catholic readers will find this Gospel particularly helpful for training in Catholic doctrine and in understanding the Church as the kingdom of God. At the same time, readers from all faith backgrounds will gain a greater understanding of Jesus' mission in Israel some two thousand years ago and find some practical insights into how his kingdom can be lived out in our own lives today.

In our walk through Christ's life, I will at times draw upon the more extensive commentary on Matthew's Gospel that I coauthored with Curtis Mitch in the Catholic Commentary on Sacred Scripture series.[1] While that commentary is a much more in-depth treatment of Matthew's Gospel, *God with Us* is meant to be a highly readable book intended to open up the treasures of Matthew's Gospel for people of all walks of life. Each chapter of this study will offer biblical reflections on particular sections of Matthew's Gospel, beginning

---

[1] Curtis Mitch and Edward Sri, *The Gospel of Matthew* (Grand Rapids, MI: Baker Academic, 2010).

with Jesus' genealogy in Matthew 1 all the way through Jesus' death and Resurrection in Matthew 27–28. These reflections attempt to place Jesus in his first-century Jewish setting and consider what Jesus' words and actions would have meant in their original context. I will build upon insights from recent historical research into the life and mission of Jesus as well as the wisdom of the saints and the Catholic tradition. When Jesus is understood in his original historical context and in the light of faith, we will see more clearly that practically every move he made is charged with great meaning and sheds light on his overall plan to build his kingdom.

Each chapter ends with some questions for group discussion or private reflection. These questions are intended to help readers interact directly with the texts from Matthew's Gospel and experience the joys of discovering rich insights in the inspired words of Scripture. There is nothing like reading and praying through the Gospels and allowing the Lord to speak to us through the sacred texts. That is why the questions are also meant to help stimulate thought and discussion on how Christ can build his kingdom in our own lives today—in our world, in our work, in our families, and, most of all, in our own hearts.

Chapter 1

The Return of the King

MATTHEW 1

FOR MOST PEOPLE, reading a biblical genealogy is about as exciting as reading the fine print in an instruction manual. Yet this is exactly how the entire New Testament begins in chapter one of Matthew's Gospel:

> The book of the genealogy of Jesus Christ, the son of David, the son of Abraham. Abraham was the father of Isaac, and Isaac the father of Jacob, and Jacob the father of Judah and his brothers, and Judah the father of Perez and Zerah . . . (Mt. 1:1–3)

I would bet that many readers today do what I did when I first looked at this genealogy: skip the long list of names and pick up again in chapter two! Even the few brave readers who survive the list of forty-two generations are nevertheless probably left wondering, "Couldn't Matthew have chosen a *better* way to begin his Gospel?"

Admittedly, being hit with a family tree of people who lived thousands of years ago doesn't seem to be the most captivating way to lure people into the story of Jesus Christ. As one New Testament scholar put it, "Let's face it: Other people's family trees are about as interesting as other people's holiday videos."[1]

If there were modern media outlets in first-century Judaism, this genealogy would have made the top story on CNN.

For a Jew in Jesus' day, however, this genealogy would have had more attention-grabbing power than the most popular video or news item trending on social media today. It would have summed up all their hopes and expectations about what God had been promising to do in their lives ever since the time of Abraham. And it would have triumphantly announced that God's plan had come to completion in their own lifetime! In fact, if there were modern media outlets in first-century Judaism, this little genealogy would have made the top story on CNN.

Let's look at Matthew's genealogy with new eyes— with the eyes of first-century Jews who would have seen their identity, history, and future encapsulated in these few verses. In the process, we will begin to see how this

[1] N.T. Wright, *Following Jesus: Biblical Reflections on Discipleship* (Grand Rapids: Eerdmans, 1995), 23.

story of Jesus, which sums up the story of Israel, has become our story—the story of the Church.

THE PROMISED "SON OF DAVID"

For the ancient Jews, a genealogy is not just a long list of names. Every name tells a story. And the name that stands out most in Jesus' genealogy is David, the great king of Israel in the Old Testament.

Consider the many ways Matthew draws attention to David and his relationship with Jesus. The very first title Matthew bestows on Jesus in the opening verse is the "Son of David" (1:1). Another link between David and Jesus is that they are the only individuals who are given titles.[2] David is described as "the king" (1:6) and Jesus is called the "Christ"—meaning "anointed one" (1:16), a title given to a Davidic king when he was anointed at his coronation. Scholars have also found Davidic imagery in verse 17, in which Matthew draws attention to the number of generations in the genealogy from Abraham to Jesus:

> [T]he generations from Abraham to David were fourteen generations, and from David to the deportation to Babylon fourteen generations, and from the deportation to Babylon to the Christ fourteen generations. (Mt. 1:17)

---

[2] On these points, I am indebted to my friend and colleague Curtis Mitch, co-author of the Ignatius Study Bible.

Here, Matthew divides all forty-two generations of the genealogy into three sets of fourteen. He is drawing our attention to the number fourteen, which is significant because David's name "adds up" to fourteen in Hebrew. Let me explain. In the Hebrew alphabet, letters are also given numeric value. The three Hebrew consonants in David's name are dwd (d = 4, w = 6), adding up to fourteen. Thus, the very structure of Matthew's genealogy centered around three sets of fourteen generations subtly proclaims Jesus to be the "thrice-Davidic Son of David."[3]

Why all this focus on David? Allusions to David would bring to mind the glory days of Israel's history, when the kingdom reached its peak in terms of its political power and influence in the world. But that's not all. God promised David and his descendants an everlasting dynasty: "your house and your kingdom shall be made sure for ever before me; your throne shall be established for ever" (2 Sam. 7:16). This dynasty would have worldwide influence: the Davidic king would rule over all the earth, nations would bow down before him, and in him all peoples would find blessing (cf. Pss. 2:8; 72:8–11, 17; 110:6). And God promised that one day, a new son of David would come—someone who would rescue God's people from their enemies, restore the kingdom, and extend its reign to all nations (Is. 11:1–10; Amos 9:11–2).

---

[3] Marshall D. Johnson, *The Purpose of the Biblical Genealogies, with Special References to the Setting of the Genealogies of Jesus* (Society for New Testament Studies, Monograph Series, 8; London: Cambridge University, 1969), 192. Interestingly, David himself appears as the 14th generation in the family tree of Saint Matthew's Gospel.

Think about the excitement an ancient Jew would have felt in reading about the great King David in this genealogy. Jesus is introduced as a "son of David" (1:1). Then the genealogy traces the descendants of Abraham down to "David the king" (Mt. 1:6) and goes on to list the kings of Judah flowing from David's line (Mt. 1:7–10). We can imagine people

> *A genealogy is not just a long list of names. Every name tells a story.*

wondering, "Could this Jesus be *the* son of David—the one for whom we've all been waiting, the one who will bring back the kingdom and free us from our enemies?"

But then in verse 11 comes a major turning point in the genealogy which issues a somber note for Jewish readers—a sudden, sharp minor chord in the genealogy's triumphant march through David's royal descendants:

> . . . and Josiah the father of Jechoniah and his brothers, at the time of the deportation to Babylon. (Mt. 1:11)

Here in this one verse, Matthew sums up six centuries of Jewish anguish, suffering, and oppression. Matthew highlights the Babylonian deportation not so much as a chronological marker, but as a signpost signaling a tragic shift in the story of Israel: the end of the Davidic monarchy. These words recall how all of Israel's hopes surrounding the Davidic kingdom were crushed in 586 BC when the Babylonians conquered Jerusalem, destroyed the Temple, and carried the people and even their king into a most humiliating exile.

This exile was not simply a painful memory from the distant past, but an abiding reality for the Jews in Jesus' day, who continued to feel the effects of this devastating loss. For most of the six centuries following the Babylonian exile, the Jewish people continued to suffer oppression under the hands of various foreign nations up to the time of Jesus, when the Romans ruled the land. For hundreds of years, the Jews were a nation without control over their own land and a people without their own king, a son of David, sitting on the throne.

The end of the kingdom was not simply a political disaster or military defeat. For a long time, God's prophets had been reminding the people that Israel's strength depended not on military might, economic wealth, or political maneuvering but on covenant faithfulness to the one true God. Israel's law taught them that if they broke their covenant relationship with Yahweh, they would suffer the curse of exile, in which even their king would be carried away by a foreign nation and God would no longer be with them (cf. Deut. 28:32–36; 31:16–18). This is exactly what happened at the time of the deportation to Babylon (cf. 2 Kings 24).

With Matthew's mention of the Babylonian exile, all the sadness, frustration, and despair that surrounded the first-century Jews' experience of suffering and oppression would ring loudly in their ears. All this is summed up in this one short verse about the exile (Matthew 1:11), and the genealogy continues these somber notes and minor chords by listing the next two generations of exiled Davidic descendants up to a man named Zerubbabel in verse 12.

God offered the Jews some hope during this period of suffering and exile. He sent his prophets to tell how a new Davidic king would be raised up—a messiah ("anointed one") who would restore the kingdom and bring about the New Covenant era in which there would be forgiveness of sins and blessing for the whole world.[4] Most first-century Jews reading Matthew's genealogy would be longing for these promises to be fulfilled.

Matthew plays upon those hopes in verse 13, where the genealogy slowly begins to change keys again. Consider the dramatic shift between verse 12 and verse 13.

In verse 12, Matthew mentions Zerubbabel, who was the last of the Davidic descendants in Matthew's genealogy recorded in the Old Testament—another tragic note. What happened to the royal line of David generations after Zerubabbel had been uncertain, for it had not been recorded in the Scriptures—until verse 13 of Matthew's Gospel. Verse 13 offers a sign of new hope, showing for the first time how the Davidic royal line continued throughout the centuries *even after Zerubbabel!* This, no doubt, would stir excitement and anticipation: the Davidic line continues! Here are the descendants of the kings! Perhaps we will find the messiah at the end of this line!

The genealogy builds a hopeful momentum as it introduces each descendent after Zerubbabel—the royal

---

[4] See, e.g., Jer. 33:15 *et seq.*; Jer. 23:1–6; Ezek. 34; Amos 9:11–12; Dan. 9:25–26; cf. Is. 45:1–5; 21–25.

men who were previously unrecorded in Scripture: Abiud, Eliakim, Azor, Zadok, Achim and so on. Finally, it reaches the peak of its crescendo when Matthew presents "Joseph the husband of Mary, of whom Jesus was born, who is called Christ" (1:16). Here, the chorus resounds at the climax of the whole genealogy: Jesus is the "Christ"—the messiah God had foretold would restore the kingdom and bring to completion his plan of blessing the entire world!

EMMANUEL: GOD WITH US

The chorus continues into verses 18–23, in which Matthew highlights two more titles for this great royal Son. First, Matthew shows us how this child's very name has great importance. He shall be called "Jesus," which literally means "God saves." Why is he given this name? Matthew tells us through the angel's explanation to Joseph: "[A]nd you shall call his name Jesus, for he will save his people from their sins" (1:21).

Here we see that Jesus' name in verse 21 is the answer to the problem of the Babylonian exile in verse 11.[5] Remember, the Jews viewed their exilic condition not simply as a political or military problem, but as a sin problem. According to their prophets and their law, it was covenant unfaithfulness that brought about their exile and oppression. Thus, Jesus ("God saves") comes

---

[5] See J. Jones, "Subverting the Textuality of Davidic Messianism: Matthew's Presentation of the Genealogy of the Davidic Title," *Catholic Biblical Quarterly* 56 (1994): 263–64.

to "save his people from their sins," thereby saving the Jews from the real exile—which is not being chained down by the Babylonians or Romans, but being enslaved to the real oppressor, the devil, who has a hold over all humanity through the chains of sin and death.

Of all the titles for Jesus that Matthew highlights, perhaps the most profound one comes right at the end of his first chapter. Jesus is called "Emmanuel," which means "God with us" (Mt. 1:23). We cannot understate how much this must have meant to ancient Jews. Ever since the first sin, when Adam and Eve "hid themselves from the presence of the Lord" (Gen. 3:8), God has been working to restore communion with sinful humanity. And God planned to use Israel as his chosen people and the Davidic king as their leader and representative in order to reach the nations and gather all people back into communion with the one true God. But without their kingdom, without a Davidic king, and still suffering under foreign domination, some first-century Jews might have wondered what happened to God's great promises for their nation and felt somewhat abandoned. Was God still with his people?

But Matthew triumphantly proclaims that the royal child at the end of the genealogy is the answer to their hearts' deepest longings. Not only is he the Christ—the anointed Davidic king who will restore the kingdom. And not only is he Jesus, the one who will save his people from their sins, he is Emmanuel—God with us. God is with his people again!

Indeed, as we shall see in subsequent reflections on Matthew's Gospel, the New Covenant that Jesus inaugurates restores communion with our heavenly Father and gives us God's presence in a way like never before: God is with us in the Church, in his Word, in the sacraments, and most intimately in the Holy Eucharist. If you want to see just how important this theme of "Emmanuel" is for Saint Matthew, turn to the very end of his Gospel. Just as "God with us" appears as the climactic name for Jesus at the end of Matthew 1, so it appears at the culmination of Matthew's entire Gospel in Jesus' last words to the apostles, promising them that he will be with them always, even to the end of time:

> Go therefore and make disciples of all nations, baptizing them in the name of the Father and of the Son and of the Holy Spirit, teaching them to observe all that I have commanded you; and lo, *I am with you always*, to the close of the age. (Mt. 28:19–20)

Questions for Discussion

1. What impressions do most people have of biblical genealogies? Why would this genealogy in Matthew 1 have grabbed the attention of first-century Jewish readers? What would it have meant to them?

2. What did the prophets say about the future son of David? Consider the following passages: Isaiah 9:2–7; Micah 5:2–4; and Jeremiah 23:1–6.

3. What are the various ways the genealogy in Matthew 1 draws attention to Jesus' being this long-awaited Davidic king? Consider the following verses: Matthew 1:1; 1:16; 1:17; and 1:13–16.

4. Read Matthew 1:22–23. At the end of the first chapter, Jesus is called "Emmanuel." What does this word mean? Why might this name for Jesus be important to the Jewish people who had been oppressed for over five hundred years?

5. Read Matthew 18:20 and 28:16–20. In what ways does Jesus continue to be with us today?

Chapter 2

Fulfilling All Prophecy

THE GOSPEL ACCOUNTS of Christ's life are like the last chapter of a great book or the last scene of a great movie.

Have you ever tried to jump in the middle of a movie that's approaching its closing scene? If you don't know the plot that went before, you're likely to be a little lost, not fully understanding the story's conclusion.

The same is true with the story of Jesus. His story is the climactic scene in a plot that has been going on from the beginning of time. Indeed, the entire life of Jesus—his birth, his preaching, his parables, his healings, his choosing the twelve apostles, his conflict with the Pharisees, his death—is all part of the dramatic conclusion to God's overarching plan from the Old Testament to prepare his people for the Messiah. If you don't know how God gradually prepares the human family from Adam to Noah to Abraham to Moses to David and the prophets, then you're likely to miss out on a lot of what Jesus said and did throughout his life as he was bringing that Old Testament story to its dramatic climax.

Matthew, more than any other Gospel, is constantly making connections to that Old Testament story. Some scholars say he makes hundreds of allusions to stories, prophecies, prayers and teachings from the Jewish Scriptures. There are two main ways Matthew does this, and it's crucial to know these two approaches if we want to follow his magnificent account of Christ's life. Matthew uses (a) *explicit fulfillment quotations* and (b) *implicit allusions* to the Old Testament story. Both approaches beautifully demonstrate how God's plan of salvation is brought to fulfillment in every little detail of Christ's life. Thankfully, both approaches are very easy to see here in the first two chapters of Matthew's Gospel—the accounts of Christ's infancy and childhood.

FULFILLMENT QUOTATIONS AND IMPLICIT ALLUSIONS

First, Matthew uses *fulfillment quotations*. This is when Matthew pauses for a moment in his storytelling and spells out for us how a prophecy is being fulfilled. You can't miss it. It's as if he's shouting out, "Hey, everyone! Did you notice what just happened here? What Jesus just did is a fulfillment of this prophecy from the Old Testament!"

How does this work? First, after telling a story from

Christ's life, *Matthew grabs our attention with a certain formulaic expression* like "This was done to fulfill what was spoken by the prophet." That wakes us up to realize that what just happened in Jesus' life is connected to an Old Testament prophecy.

But how do we know which prophecy Matthew has in mind? What if we don't know the Old Testament well and don't consider ourselves experts in biblical prophecy? Not to worry. Matthew is going to do a second thing that makes it very easy for us. We don't need to thumb through our Bibles searching through hundreds of Old Testament promises and prophecies because *Matthew is going to quote the passage he has in mind*. It's as if he cuts and pastes Old Testament prophecies right into his Gospel account for our convenience!

We've already seen one example of this. When telling how Joseph learns about the Virgin Mary conceiving Christ by the power of the Holy Spirit, Matthew underscores how this was foreshadowed in the Old Testament. He writes, "All this took place to fulfill what the Lord had spoken by the prophet" (1:22). That's *the formulaic expression* used to grab our attention and help us realize a prophecy is being fulfilled. Then, Matthew *quotes the prophecy* he has in mind, which is from Isaiah 7:14: "Behold, a virgin shall conceive and bear a son, and his name shall be called Emmanuel" (1:23). Isn't that easy? Matthew spells it all out for us. He announces a prophecy is being fulfilled and then includes

> *Matthew, more than any other Gospel, is constantly making connections to the Old Testament.*

a quote from the prophecy itself. Thank you, Matthew!

Another example of this is when the magi come to King Herod inquiring about a newborn king of the Jews. Herod asks the chief priests and scribes to tell him where the Messiah was expected to be born. They tell him, "In Bethlehem" and then go on to say, "for so it is written by the prophet"—which is *the formulaic expression* to draw attention to the fact that a prophecy is being fulfilled. And then he *quotes the particular prophecy* in mind—a prophecy from the Book of Micah: "And you, O Bethlehem, in the land of Judah, are by no means least among the rulers of Judah; for from you shall come a ruler" (Mt. 2:5–6; cf. Mic. 5:1; 2 Sam. 5:2).

Do you see how easy Matthew makes it for us with these fulfillment quotations? Matthew uses this simple approach ten times in his Gospel, and half of those fulfillment quotations are found up front in Matthew 1–2 in the stories of Christ's infancy and childhood (Mt. 1:22–23; 2:5–6; 2:15; 2:17–18; 2:23).

Most of the time, however, Matthew doesn't make it so easy. Some scholars point out that Matthew is constantly making subtle allusions to an Old Testament story and assumes you know the background and will easily make the connection. He assumes you as the reader know the Old Testament like young people today know lyrics from their favorite songs and lines from their favorite shows and movies.

If I say to someone who has grown up with American pop culture, "May the force be with you," they're likely to think about Luke Skywalker and the Star Wars movies. But someone unfamiliar with those films will have no idea what I'm talking about. Similarly, if you hear people at the start of a baseball game sing, "Oh say can you see by the dawn's early light," you know they're singing the USA's national anthem. But if you didn't know anything about American culture, you might be very confused and wonder, "Why is everyone in full chorus asking me about my eyesight in the early morning hours?"

Matthew uses this simple approach to prophecy fulfillment ten times in his Gospel.

The ancient Jews didn't have baseball, Hollywood, iTunes, or Netflix. Their popular culture was shaped by the Scriptures. The stories of the Bible are what permeated their daily lives—what they talked about, what they heard in the Synagogue, what they pondered in prayer, what they celebrated and re-enacted in various feasts throughout the year. Matthew assumes that if he just quotes one line from a story or makes a few simple allusions, you'll make the connection just like we do when we hear famous lines from our favorite songs, movies, and shows today.

Take, for example, the Christmas story about the magi. Matthew 2 tells of magi from the east who see a star over Israel and come to Herod in Jerusalem searching for a newborn king. Herod tells the magi to look for the Christ child in Bethlehem, saying, "Go and search diligently for the child, and when you have found him bring me word, that I too may come and worship him" (2:8). But he doesn't really want to pay homage to the child. He just wants to know where the child is so he can kill him.

When the magi find the royal child, they offer him luxurious gifts fit for a king: gold, frankincense (an expensive perfume), and myrrh (an exotic spice). They fall down to worship him. But instead of reporting back to Herod, they return home by another way (Mt. 2:10–12).

This story of the magi would have been very familiar to the Jews in the first century. It would have sounded like a "re-make" of an old song they had heard many times before: a wicked king, trying to use magi from the east to bring harm to Jesus, but the magi not going along with the king's plan and instead blessing and honoring Jesus. That would remind them of a famous story in their tradition: the story of Balak and Balaam in the Book of Numbers 22–24.

Balak was the wicked king of Moab who wanted to bring harm to the Israelites who were approaching the Promised Land. Balak calls upon a man named Balaam, a wise man from the East, to put a curse on the people of Israel. But every time he tries to curse the Israelites, God intervenes and words of blessing come out of his mouth. Instead of cursing Israel, he blesses Israel!

All this, of course, foreshadows the events surrounding Christ's birth. Just as the wicked King Balaak attempts to employ a seer from the east named Balaam to harm Israel, so the wicked King Herod tries to use the magi from the east in his plot to discover where the Christ child is. Just as Balaam didn't cooperate with Balak's plan, blessing Israel instead of cursing the people, so the magi didn't assist in Herod's plan, paying homage to the baby Jesus and not revealing his location to Herod.

But the most fascinating connection is found in

how the story of Balak and Balaam ends. After three attempts to curse Israel, Balaam finds God's speech taking over once again, but this time, Balaam utters a prophecy about some great king coming to Israel in the distant future:

> I see him, but not now;
> I behold him, but not near;
> A star shall come forth out of Jacob,
> And a scepter shall rise out of Israel.
> (Num. 24:17)

Let's unpack the symbolism in this prophecy. The scepter is a royal staff, symbolizing a king who will one day come to Israel. And according to this prophecy, a *star* will be the sign of the king's coming. So when the magi see the star in the direction of Israel, their coming to Jerusalem in search of a king would make perfect sense to the first century Israelite—it's just what Balaam had prophesied long ago. In this sense, the magi in the Christmas story are like successors to Balaam in that they worship the king whom Balaam foretold many centuries ago.[1]

NEW MOSES, NEW EXODUS

This is not the only time in Matthew 2 when we find subtle allusions to the Old Testament stories. Matthew's

---

[1] William Davies and Dale Alison, *The Gospel according to Saint Matthew* (Edinburgh: T&T Clark, 1988), 1:229.

account of the horrific scene known as the "Massacre of the Holy Innocents" is another example.

Matthew tells of Herod's decree to kill the young male children around Bethlehem. Jesus escapes with his parents to Egypt only to come back to Israel later, after an angel appears to Joseph, telling him, "...those who sought the child's life are dead" (Mt. 2:20).

All this would remind ancient Jews of the story of Moses in the Book of Exodus. Just as Jesus was born during *Herod's murderous decree*, so Moses was born during *Pharaoh murderous declaration* that every male child born to the Israelites should be thrown into the Nile River. And just as *the Christ child escaped death by fleeing to Egypt* where he was raised for a bit, so the baby *Moses escapes death by being raised in the highest Egyptian household* when Pharaoh's daughter takes Moses as her own child. Finally, Moses will return to his fellow Israelites when God appears to him in a burning bush, saying, *"all the men who were seeking your life are dead"* (Ex. 4:19). These are almost the exact same words the angel spoke to Joseph when Jesus was to return to the land of Israel: "Rise, take the child and his mother, and go to the land of Israel, *for those who sought the child's life are dead*" (Mt. 2:20).

Right from his birth, Jesus is being presented as a New Moses, which is an important paradigm for understanding what Christ's life is all about. Just as Moses liberated the people from slavery in Egypt, so Jesus will lead the people in a New Exodus, liberating them from sin—a theme, we will see, that Matthew will develop more throughout his Gospel.

Another subtle connection Matthew makes with the Old Testament is found in St. Joseph, the husband of Mary. Matthew points out a number of details that would remind us of another biblical hero with the same name: the patriarch Joseph in the Book of Genesis.

Just as St. Joseph is introduced as a son of Jacob, so the patriarch Joseph of old has a father named Jacob (Mt. 1:16). Just as St. Joseph suffers unjustly under Herod's terror, so the patriarch Joseph suffers unjustly at the hands of his brothers who sell him into slavery.

Both Josephs also are known for their dreams. St. Joseph is given important dreams through which God guides him to take Mary as his wife, to flee to Egypt, to come back to Israel, and to avoid returning to Judah. This would recall the patriarch Joseph who was famous for having dreams in his childhood about his future rise to glory and then, in his adult years, interpreting other people's dreams like Pharaoh's visions about seven years of abundant harvest in the land followed by seven years of severe famine. Finally, both Josephs were known for protecting their families—St. Joseph protected his family from Herod's massacre while the patriarch Joseph saved his family from famine.

The magi and Balaam, the baby Jesus and baby Moses, St. Joseph the husband of Mary and the patriarch Joseph. These are just a few of the plethora of parallels between the story of the Old Testament and the story of Jesus that are found in Matthew's Gospel. Be on the lookout for these kinds of allusions every step of the way, for Matthew is constantly making connections to Old Testament people, events, stories, laws, prayers, and prophecies and he assumes his readers will follow his moves. The more we know about the Old Testament, therefore, the more we will track with the Gospel accounts of Christ's life. To assist in this process, we will continue to unpack that key Old Testament background so that we can more fully appreciate all that Jesus says and does in his ministry.

QUESTIONS FOR DISCUSSION

1. What were your impressions of the Old Testament before reading this chapter?

2. Why is the Old Testament so important for understanding the story of Jesus?

3. We saw in this chapter how Matthew makes several connections to the Old Testament. Which connection impressed you the most? Why?

4. How does Matthew's approach to the Jewish Scriptures change the way you view the Old Testament now? What are some things you can do to know that Old Testament story better?

Chapter 3

The King's Anointing

THE FIRST TIME I visited the Jordan River—the place where John the Baptist began his ministry—I couldn't help but think that the prophet could have chosen a much better place to launch his movement and prepare the people for the Messiah.

The Jordan River flows through a barren wilderness into the lowest point on the entire face of the earth, some 1,200 feet below sea level. To get there, crowds would have to trek several hours down through the rugged desert terrain with the hot, piercing sun relentlessly beating down on their backs.

Who would want to go all the way down *there* to hear John the Baptist? It seems that the capital city of Jerusalem would have been a much better site for attracting listeners. Or maybe the highly populated region of Galilee. But the empty wilderness and the Jordan River basin?

Yet, for the ancient Jews, the Jordan River valley was much more than a desolate wilderness. It was the very place where they expected God to do great things for Israel again. And this makes all the difference for understanding the mission of John the Baptist and his fateful encounter with Jesus at that river.

The Jews knew that amazing things happened at the Jordan River. This is the place where the prophet Elisha cured Naaman, servant of the King of Syria (2 Kings 5:1–14). This is where the prophet Elijah was taken up into heaven in a fiery chariot (2 Kings 2:1–10). But most of all, this river would bring to mind the most important event in Israel's history—the Exodus.

To this day, Jews annually recall the story of the Exodus, retelling how God freed the Israelites from slavery in Egypt, led them through the Red Sea, and guided them in the desert for forty years. The climax of this drama comes when Joshua led the Israelites through the Jordan River and into the land God had promised them. It was then that Israel began its life anew as a nation in the land of Canaan.

As such, the Jordan River valley became a rich symbol for new beginnings and new life. It expressed Israel's hopes for the future, hopes for a new type of exodus, when God would once again free his people from their pagan enemies as he did back in the time of Moses and Joshua. In fact, the prophets foretold how the desert would be the stage where Israel would return to God and their covenant would be renewed. For example, the prophet Hosea described how sinful Israel would come back to Yahweh like an unfaithful wife returning to her husband. And this spousal reunion would take place in the desert:

> Therefore, behold, I will allure her, and bring her into the wilderness, and speak tenderly to her. . . . And I will make for you a covenant. . . . I will betroth you to me for ever. (Hos. 2:14, 18–19)

This is why John the Baptist called the people out into the wilderness to be baptized in the Jordan. Such an action would signal the beginning of all that the Jews had been hoping for. This was a symbolic action, ritually reenacting the Exodus. Just like their ancestors, the Jews following John the Baptist went out into the wilderness, passed through the Jordan, and reentered the Promised Land. And they came out on the other side with all their hopes for a fresh start—hopes for freedom, this time, however, not from the Egyptians but from their current oppressors, the Romans. One can imagine the great enthusiasm and anticipation surrounding John the Baptist's movement. It's no wonder John had little trouble attracting so many people!

This was a powerful symbolic action, ritually reenacting the Exodus.

WHO CARES ABOUT HIS FASHION?

Now John wore a garment of camel's hair, and a leather girdle around his waist. . . (Mt. 3:4)

Matthew's Gospel does not tell us much about what John the Baptist preached to the crowds at the Jordan. In fact, he only quotes nine words from John's actual preaching: "Repent, for the kingdom of heaven is at hand" (Mt. 3:2). It might seem odd that Matthew uses more words describing the type of clothes John the Baptist was wearing than he does telling us about the content of John's message. However, anyone familiar with the Old Testament would find great significance in John's being garbed in camel's hair and a leather girdle around his waist—for this is exactly what the great prophet Elijah was known for wearing (cf. 2 Kings 1:8).

This was significant because the Jews had been waiting for Elijah's return. Consider the very last prophetic words addressed to Israel in the Old Testament. Malachi was the last prophet sent to Israel and, in his final prophetic utterance, he said Elijah would in some way return to Israel before the time of the Messiah (cf. Mal. 4:5). For centuries after Malachi, the Jewish people waited in silence with no prophet being sent to them (cf. 1 Mac. 9:27; 14:41). These last words about Elijah's reappearance were left echoing in their ears, as they anticipated the coming of Elijah and the Messiah who would follow after him.

When John began his ministry dressed with Elijah-styled camel's hair and leather girdle, this signaled to the Jews that he was playing the part of the returned Elijah. Indeed, Jesus himself later recognized this, saying, "For all the prophets and the law prophesied until John; and if you are willing to accept it, he is Elijah who is to come" (Mt. 11:13–14). Acting as the new Elijah,

John the Baptist announced that Malachi's prophecy was coming to fulfillment and that the time of the Messiah was just around the corner!

But John and Elijah had much more in common than clothing. Both John and Elijah were great prophets. Both challenged evil kings to change their wicked ways, and both were persecuted for doing so. The most striking parallel is the fact that both John and Elijah prepared the way for prophets with even greater ministries than their own. Before Elijah was taken up to heaven, he gave his successor, Elisha, a double portion of his spirit (2 Kings 2:9, 15), which was the launching pad for Elisha's ministry. Elisha then went on to do even greater things than his predecessor Elijah had done. For example, Elisha miraculously cleansed a leper (2 Kings 5:1–19), raised a child from the dead (2 Kings 4:32–37), and multiplied barley loaves to feed a crowd (2 Kings 4:42–44).

All this, of course, prefigures John the Baptist and Jesus. When John baptized Jesus, the Spirit descended upon him like a dove, and this event served as the foundation for his public ministry. Jesus then went on to do even greater works than John the Baptist. Like Elisha, Jesus also cleansed lepers (Mt. 8:2–4), raised a child from the dead (Mt. 9:23–25), and multiplied barley loaves to feed the multitudes (Jn. 6:9–14; cf. Mt. 14:15–21; 15:32–38).

The most significant parallel is the place where Elijah passed on his prophetic mission to Elisha: the Jordan River (2 Kings 2:6–14). At the Jordan, Elijah transferred his ministry to his successor, Elisha. It was also there that the new Elijah—John the Baptist—

passed the baton to Jesus, who then began his public ministry as the new Elisha.

THE MESSIAH'S ARRIVAL

With this background, we can appreciate why John the Baptist would attract such a large following. His baptism ministry at the Jordan instilled hope for a new type of exodus, this time bringing liberation from the Romans. And his appearing like Elijah signaled that Israel's long-awaited Messiah-King was soon to arrive on the scene to lead the people to freedom and restore the kingdom.

Nevertheless, John made it clear that he himself was not the exodus leader. He himself was not the Messiah:

> I baptize you with water for repentance, but he who is coming after me is mightier than I, whose sandals I am not worthy to carry; he will baptize you with the Holy Spirit and with fire. (Mt. 3:11)

John viewed himself simply as a predecessor, preparing the way for the Messiah.

But then one day, it happened. The Messiah arrived. "Jesus came forth from Galilee to the Jordan to John, to be baptized by him" (Mt. 3:13). What an amazing encounter that must have been! For John, this meeting meant the culmination of his entire career as the prophet who prepared the people for their king. For Jesus, however, it marked the very beginning of his mission as the Messiah.

Jesus' baptism can be seen as his anointing as king and his inauguration as Israel's Messiah.

The word "messiah" ("anointed one" in Hebrew) was often used in the Old Testament to describe the Davidic king who was anointed with oil as he assumed his royal office.

His clothing signaled to the Jews that he was playing the part of the returned Elijah.

The Jews also used the word "messiah" to designate the future anointed king who would carry out the new exodus and restore the Davidic kingdom.

When Jesus comes to the Jordan to be baptized, something happens that would signal to the careful observer that this event marks the beginning of Jesus' ministry as the hoped-for Messiah:

> [T]he heavens were opened and he saw the Spirit of God descending like a dove, and alighting on him; and lo, a voice from heaven, saying, "This is my beloved Son, with whom I am well pleased." (Mt. 3:16–17)

The Spirit's descending on Jesus calls to mind how the Spirit fell upon the Jewish kings of the Old Testament when they were anointed. For example, Samuel told Saul that one of the signs that he was truly anointed king was that "the spirit of the Lord will come mightily upon you" (1 Sam. 10:6). Similarly when Samuel anointed David as king, "the Spirit of the Lord came mightily upon David from that day forward (1 Sam. 16:13).

It is not surprising that the Jewish people expected the future Messiah-King to receive the Spirit in a similar way. In fact, the prophet Isaiah made this very point when he foretold how the messianic son of David would receive the Spirit upon him as a source of wisdom, understanding, counsel, and might (Is. 11:2). So the Spirit's coming upon Jesus at the Jordan could be seen as a royal event recalling the anointing of Israel's great kings, including the Messiah.

The voice from heaven saying, "This is my beloved Son, with whom I am well pleased" (Mt. 3:17), also has messianic overtones. These words bring to mind an important figure in the Book of Isaiah: the Servant of the Lord, who in some Jewish circles was associated with Israel's hopes for the Messiah.[1]

Isaiah foretold how God would send this Servant to suffer for Israel's sins and bring about the blessings of the New Covenant (Is. 40–55). God would send his Spirit upon his Servant and rejoice in him: "Behold my servant . . . in whom my soul delights; I have put my Spirit upon him" (Is. 42:1). In Matthew 3, the voice from heaven draws from this language of Isaiah, showing how Isaiah's prophecy is fulfilled in Jesus' baptism, when the Spirit descends upon him and the Father declares that he is "well pleased" in him (Mt. 3:17).

What is significant for our purposes is how this

---

[1] Some Jews seem to have interpreted the servant figure in a messianic sense. For example, Zechariah 3:8 describes the messianic "branch" figure (cf. Is. 11:1; Jer. 23:5; 33:15) as "my servant." For further commentary, see N.T. Wright, *Jesus and the Victory of God* (Minneapolis: Fortress Press, 1996), 588–90.

coming of the Spirit upon Jesus is Jesus' anointing. Isaiah himself specifically described the Servant's reception of the Spirit as an anointing: "The Spirit of the Lord God is upon me, because the Lord has anointed me" (Is. 61:1).[2] And this is how Peter eventually interpreted Jesus' baptism, saying, "God anointed Jesus of Nazareth with the Holy Spirit and with power" (Acts 10:38).

When Jesus comes out of the Jordan, therefore, he comes out as Israel's royal Messiah-King anointed by the Holy Spirit. Now as the truly "Anointed One," Jesus is ready to begin his messianic mission of building the kingdom. Here we can see that the Jordan River in the wilderness certainly was a place of new beginnings!

---

[2] See Donald Hagner, Matthew 1–13 in *Word Biblical Commentary*, vol. 33a (Dallas: Word Books, 1993), 58; Timothy Gray, "Holy Oil in the Desert: The Baptism and Anointing of Jesus" *Lay Witness* (September 1998): 32.

QUESTIONS FOR DISCUSSION

1. Imagine being a Jew in the first century and hearing about John the Baptist's ministry. What would be the symbolism of his taking people out into the desert and leading them through the Jordan River? What hopes might he be stirring in the Jewish people's hearts?

2. John the Baptist challenged the people to "repent," which means to "turn around." The idea is to turn away from sin and turn back toward God. What are some ways we can put this into practice? How can we make repenting more of a part of our daily lives?

3. In what ways does the Old Testament prophet Elijah prefigure John the Baptist? (See Malachi 4:5; 2 Kings 1:8; and Matthew 3:4.)

4. In what ways might the prophet Elisha (Elijah's successor) prefigure Jesus? Consider the following verses: 2 Kings 5:1–19; 4:32–38; 4:42–44; 2:6–15.

5. At Jesus' baptism, he heard the Father's voice say, "This is my beloved son." By virtue of your baptism, you have Christ in you and were made a beloved child of God. Close your eyes and picture God the Father saying the same of you: "This is my beloved son/daughter." How much do you realize how beloved you really are in God's eyes? How might realizing the Father's amazing, unconditional love for us more impact the way we approach our relationship with God?

Chapter 4

Battle in the Desert

JESUS BEGAN his career with a very bold opening move.

Notice how Jesus did not start his public ministry by teaching in the synagogue or preaching on the streets. Nor did he begin by performing miraculous works like healing the sick, walking on the water, or raising the dead. Rather, the very first thing Jesus chose to do was to confront the devil.

After his baptism in the Jordan River, Jesus traveled out into the desert to fast and pray for forty days, and there he was tempted three times by Satan. What was the significance of this intense duel between the King of Kings and the prince of this world? We will see how Jesus fights his first battle as the Messiah-King, but he does so in a way that may have caught many first-century Jews by surprise.

THE LION KING

In Matthew 3, Jesus' baptism marked the beginning of his messianic mission. There at the Jordan, the Spirit descended upon him, just as the Spirit descended on Israel's monarchs when they were anointed as kings. As we saw in the previous chapter, Jesus was thus identified as the "Anointed One" or "Messiah." But what did it mean to be the Messiah? What were Jews expecting the Messiah-King to do?

Israel's kings were often associated with fighting Israel's battles. The Jews thought that a Messiah-King would be part of God's plan to restore Israel and free them from the pagan nations.

This, after all, is what the great Israelite kings of old had done. For example, King David defeated Goliath and the Philistines. King Hezekiah reigned as king when the Assyrian armies were turned away. King Josiah lost his life in a battle against the Egyptians. The great kings of Israel were known for protecting God's people from the oppression of their pagan neighbors.

Looking to the future, the Psalms and the prophets foretold how God would send another great king to do the same. This future son of David would establish his dominion by triumphing over the pagan nations. From the fall of the Davidic monarchy (586 BC) to the time of Jesus, these scriptural texts fueled Jewish hopes for a renewed Davidic dynasty. God would send a new king who would free the Israelites from their enemies, reestablish Israel in the Promised Land, and bring blessing to the world (Pss. 2:8; 72:8–11, 17; 110:6; Is. 9:1–7; 11:1–10; Ezek. 34; Dan. 9).

A HOLY WAR?

This certainly was good news for Jews in Jesus' day. After centuries of foreign domination, they longed for the renewal of the Davidic dynasty and anxiously anticipated the coming of the great king who would liberate Israel.

Some Jews in the century before Jesus even put their hopes down in writing, creating texts of their own that described how God would send a king who would lead them into triumph over their enemies. They told stories about how this king would smash the Gentiles like a potter's jar crushed to pieces. The messiah would come out of the forest like a lion to deliver the faithful Jews from the hands of the Romans. Indeed, this "holy war" theology surrounded many Jewish longings for the restoration of Israel. But was this the type of liberation Jesus would offer?

Like the great kings who went before him, Jesus as the Messiah-King did enter into a battle of his own. But his battle was very different from what many of his contemporaries were expecting. Instead of confronting the Romans—who were the oppressors of the Jews in Jesus' day—Jesus marched into the desert to combat a much fiercer opponent: *the devil.*

The account in Matthew 4 of Jesus' overcoming the three temptations of the devil would remind the careful reader that the real enemy of Israel was much bigger than the Roman Empire or any other pagan nation. The true enemy was the power of sin and Satan. This might have come as a surprise to a number of Jewish leaders who focused on resisting Rome and who were anticipating a Messiah who would lead them in battle against their oppressors.

However, by beginning his public ministry with a showdown with the devil, Jesus shows us what type of Messiah-King he will be. It is true that he was coming to start a revolution, but it was not a militaristic one. His revolution was internal, inside the hearts and minds of God's people, freeing them from the bondage of sin.

Here, Jesus is simply acting in accordance with what the Jewish law and prophets said about Israel's situation in the first century. Israel's suffering under foreign occupation was actually a symptom of a much deeper illness. Unfaithfulness to God brought on the exile and the fall of the Davidic monarchy. To focus on driving out the Romans would be to miss the point. Violent revolution would not solve the problem. As one New Testament scholar explains, "to drive out paganism with paganism's weapons is already to lose the battle."[1]

Jesus marched into the desert to combat a much fiercer opponent: the devil.

Jesus came not to fight the Romans, but to treat the root of the problem: the sin of Israel and the sin of all humanity. If sin is conquered, Israel will be truly free. And that is what Jesus sets out to do in the desert.

As the Messiah-King, Jesus would have been viewed by his Jewish followers as their representative. Through-

---

[1] N.T. Wright, *Jesus: The New Way* (Worcester, MA: Christian History Institute, 1998), 52.

out Israel's history, the king was considered an embodiment of the whole nation. So closely was the king associated with his people that what happened to the king could be said to have happened to the people as a whole. For example, when the king was faithful to the covenant with Yahweh, the entire nation received God's blessings. But when the king sinned greatly, the whole nation suffered for his infidelity. The king represented the people.

This helps us to understand Jesus' temptations in the desert. As Israel's royal representative, Jesus experienced the same trials Israel did during the Exodus. What happened to Israel in the time of Moses happened to Jesus in the first century.

The fact that Jesus spent forty days in the desert shows how he symbolically relived the story of Israel's forty years in the wilderness during the Exodus. Furthermore, upon closer examination of Jesus' three temptations, we will see that Jesus faced the same trials Israel faced in the desert, entering into the drama of Israel's weaknesses and failings during their pilgrimage to the Promised Land.[2]

But then Jesus gave that story a surprise ending. Instead of stumbling like the ancient people of God did, he proved himself to be a faithful Israelite. Jesus remained faithful precisely where Israel had been unfaithful. As such, Jesus symbolically unties the knot of Israel's sin and "pre-enacts" what he ultimately will

---

[2] Cf. Jack Dean Kingsbury, *Matthew as Story* (Philadelphia: Fortress Press, 1988), 55.

do for Israel on the Cross: conquer sin and defeat the devil. This is the real battle Jesus fights and the real liberation he offers.

Let's take a closer look at how the three temptations of Jesus relate to the first three major trials of Israel in the Exodus. Here we will see that the failings of Israel are symbolically overcome by Jesus' victory over the devil.

Israel's first test: The first of Israel's trials involved hunger. After Moses parted the Red Sea and led the Israelites out of Egypt and into the desert, the people celebrated their newfound freedom. However, they soon faced another problem: how would they find food in this desert? Their rejoicing quickly turned into panic. Instead of trusting in God to provide, the people turned against Moses, saying "you have brought us out into this wilderness to kill this whole assembly with hunger" (Ex. 16:3).

Jesus' first test: Similarly, Jesus faced *hunger* in his first temptation as the devil tried to get him to use his power to break his forty days of fasting. The Father sent the Spirit to lead Jesus into the desert to pray and fast for forty days. For Jesus to turn the stones into bread would be to exercise his messianic authority for his own self-interest and thus depart from the Father's will. Unlike the Israelites, who doubted that God would provide for their needs in the wilderness, Jesus does not waver from trusting the Father. He quotes Deuteronomy 8:3 (a passage that brings to mind the story of Israel's first test), saying "Man shall not live by bread alone" (Mt. 4:4). As the people's royal representative, Jesus overcomes the first major fall of Israel in the desert.

Israel's second test: The second trial involved Israel putting God "to the test." After God provided for Israel's nourishment by sending them bread from heaven (manna), the people soon faced another dilemma: How were they going to find water to drink in the desert? Once again, instead of putting their trust in Yahweh to provide for their needs, they doubted him and accused Moses of orchestrating a vicious plot against them: "Why did you bring us up out of Egypt, to kill us and our children and our cattle with thirst?" (Ex. 17:3). God responded by giving them water from a rock, and he named the place of this second ordeal "Massah," which means "place of testing." There, the people unjustly tested God's trustworthiness, which is absolute and would not be questioned by the truly faithful Israelite.

Jesus' second test. This corresponds to Jesus' second temptation when the devil challenged him to throw himself down from the pinnacle of the Temple to see if God's angels would really save him. Satan said to Jesus, "If you are the Son of God, throw yourself down; for it is written, 'He will give his angels charge of you'" (Mt. 4:6). Unlike the Israelites at Massah, Jesus refused to test God

Jesus experienced the same trials Israel did during the Exodus.

on this or any other issue. Jesus had absolute confidence in the Father and had no desire to test him. This is why he viewed this second temptation as parallel to Israel's second trial in the desert. He responds to the devil by quoting part of Deuteronomy 6:16. When we consider the verse as a whole, we see that Jesus had Israel's second testing at Massah in mind: "You shall not put the Lord your God to the test, *as you tested him at Massah*" (Deut. 6:16). As such, Jesus overcomes Israel's second failing by refusing to test God in this second temptation.

Israel's third test. The last temptation of Israel involved *worshipping a false god.* This came in the golden calf episode at Mount Sinai. After Moses left the people for forty days to go up the mountain and receive the Ten Commandments, the people down below did not know what happened to their leader and feared he had died. Failing to trust Yahweh again, they built an idol in the shape of a golden calf, putting their trust in an Egyptian pagan deity.

Jesus' third test. Similarly, in the third test, Satan tempted Jesus to *worship him* in exchange for all the kingdoms of the world. Jesus refused to worship a false god and responded by alluding to Deuteronomy 6:13–14, saying "You shall worship the Lord your God and him only shall you serve" (Mt. 4:10). In this third temptation, Jesus overcomes Israel's sin of idolatry.

THE VICTORY OF JESUS

As the first act of his messiahship, Jesus' victory over the devil sets the tone for the rest of his public ministry. Most of Jesus' subsequent actions—his healings, forgiving people's sins, or exorcisms—can be seen as repercussions of his initial triumph over the devil in the desert. Jesus will go from town to town carrying out his victory over the devil in the lives of the people he meets. In touching the lives of the sick, the crippled, the blind, or the great sinners and demoniacs, Jesus frees them from the power and effects of sin. All this, of course, points to Jesus' work on the Cross, where he definitively conquers the prince of this world and wins salvation for all humanity (cf. Jn. 12:31).

The Catholic Church's annual celebration of Lent helps us experience the victory of Jesus in our own lives today. Each year, in the forty days of Lent, Christians participate in Jesus' forty days of prayer, fasting, and trial in the desert. Through our prayer and mortification, we too prepare to battle sin. But the question we must ask ourselves—in Lent or any other time of the year—is whether we will be like Israel in the desert, failing to put our trust in God, or like Jesus, faithful to our heavenly Father, so that we may experience the abundant blessings of the victory of Jesus on Easter Sunday.

QUESTIONS FOR DISCUSSION

1. In this chapter, we saw how in the Exodus story Israel did not trust in God to provide for their needs. They fell three times in the desert. But Jesus had full confidence in the Father and resisted the three temptations of the devil.

- What are some areas in our own lives where we might lack confidence in God, where it is difficult to let go and trust in God to provide for us?
- Why is it sometimes difficult to trust in God?
- Read Matthew 6:25–33. What do these verses tell us about God's fatherly care for us?
- In light of these verses, how can we be more like Jesus, confidently placing our lives in the Father's hands?

2. How might the three tests of Israel in the desert relate to the same three tests Jesus faces in the desert in Matthew 4? Consider the following passages: Exodus 16:1–3 and Matthew 4:1–4; Exodus 17:1–7 and Matthew 4:5–7 (recall that the location where Israel's test took place was named "massah," which literally means "place of testing"); and Exodus 32:1–4 and Matthew 4:8–10.

3. What does it mean to "put the Lord to the test?" How might we be tempted to not trust the Lord to provide for our needs and put him to the test?

4. In the third test, Jesus was tempted with a most terrible form of idolatry, the worship of the devil. But any time we seek our salvation, fulfillment, security and identity in anything less than God, we make it an idol. What are some "idols" we might be tempted to worship today?

Chapter 5

The Challenge of the Kingdom

MATTHEW 5 – 7

"Love your enemy." "Blessed are the merciful." "Turn the other cheek."

With these famous words from the Sermon on the Mount, Jesus was not simply setting forth a lofty ethical standard that helps us be "nice" people. He was giving a very specific, countercultural challenge to the people of his day—a message that would have turned their world upside down. Jesus was offering a new vision, a new vision for what it meant to be God's people.

The Jews in Jesus' day were facing a national crisis. Roman rulers controlled their land, took their money, and raped their women. Many of the Jewish priests and local leaders were assassinated and replaced by hand-picked appointments from Rome or Herod. Thousands of Jews who tried to resist Roman rule quickly paid the severe price of death.

This oppressive environment created numerous challenges for those who were striving to remain loyal to God's covenant. According to the Torah, God alone was king and he would rule his people through a descendant of King David. No foreigner was to rule over the Jews (Deut. 17:15). So what was a good Jew to do? Was it okay to go along with the Roman authorities, or would submitting to Caesar, Pilate, and Herod betray Yahweh's lordship?

Then came the question of taxes and tithes. With the Romans imposing heavy tax burdens, it would be quite difficult for many Jews to pay both the taxes to Caesar and the tithe, which their own law required them to give to God. So should one be faithful to Rome or to Yahweh?

Also, there was the risk of assimilation. When the Romans imported thousands of their own citizens, with their gentile practices and lifestyles, right into the midst of Jewish society, it became increasingly difficult for Jews to maintain their identity as God's holy people set apart from the nations. How to maintain covenant faithfulness and Jewish identity in these difficult circumstances was a critical question in the time of Jesus.

The Jewish people responded to this crisis in different ways. While most believed that one day God would rescue those who remained faithful to the covenant, there were diverse opinions about who those faithful

Jews would be. One burning question in first-century Judaism was: what does it mean to be a true, loyal Jew during this time of oppression?

One group, *the Pharisees,* believed faithfulness meant imitating God's holiness in a particular way. In Hebrew, "holy" literally means "set apart" or "separated," so the Pharisees thought the way to imitate God's holiness was to separate themselves from anything or anyone that was unholy. They did this through strict obser-vance of the laws in a way that would clearly distinguish themselves from their gentile or sinful neighbors. They avoided certain types of foods, certain types of animals, certain types of utensils and, most of all, certain types of people, such as sinners, tax collectors, and Gentiles (non-Jews). Little details such as these—what you ate, how you ate it, and with whom you ate—were all-pow-erful political and religious symbols. These were sym-bolic ways of expressing faithfulness to God's covenant in the midst of an unclean culture. They were ways of saying, "I am not like the sinners. I am not like the pagans. I am a true Jew, a part of God's faithful people."

The Essenes were another group who emphasized separateness—but to an even greater degree. They called for separation from society altogether. With Roman occupation and corrupt Jewish leaders in Je-rusalem, remaining holy within society was no longer a possibility. So, many of the Essenes withdrew to the desert, where they established a monastic-like commu-nity, claiming to be the only Jews left who were still faithful to God's covenant.

Other Jews believed holiness could be obtained only

zealots

by driving the Romans out of the land. *The revolutionaries* stressed that only Yahweh was meant to be king over Israel. To submit to Caesar or Herod would be to reject God's role as Israel's true king. That's why some Jews were ready to take up arms against the Romans when the time was right.

This was the complex stage which Jesus entered when he began his kingdom movement in Galilee, preaching, "Repent, for the kingdom of heaven is at hand" (Mt. 4:17).

THE SERMON ON THE MOUNT

From the start, Jesus' public ministry took off like lightning. He gathered disciples, and crowds from all over Galilee and beyond flocked to see him. Why was he so popular? His message and his actions said it all: the long-awaited kingdom was now arriving (Mt. 4:17, 23–25). Jesus was offering a message the Jews were longing to hear. With eager anticipation, many Jews began to place their hopes in him to rescue them from their enemies and restore the kingdom to Israel. No wonder Jesus' fame spread throughout the region so rapidly!

After attracting this large following, Jesus decided to lead his disciples up a mountain in Galilee for a special teaching about the kingdom, and the crowds followed. This action itself might have led some of his followers to ponder what might happen next. In those days, the hill country of Galilee was sometimes a refuge for Jewish revolutionaries who were plotting their assaults against foreign oppressors. The caves in those hills made for good hiding places. Not too long before this, a group of bandits had hidden in the Galilean hills during a fierce conflict with King Herod.

So when Jesus led his followers up a mountain in Galilee, some may have been wondering whether he was going to start some type of revolt of his own—like Judas the Galilean had done in the Galilean hill country one generation earlier. Was Jesus going to make a claim to be Israel's king and lead the people in a fight for the kingdom? The crowd waited for him to speak.

Jesus began his teaching that day with a startling message. He introduced an unexpected lineup of people who would be blessed in the kingdom he was building: "Blessed are the merciful ... Blessed are the peacemakers ... Blessed are those who are persecuted" (Mt. 5:7, 9–10).

What a shock! What kind of kingdom movement was *this*? Jesus seemed to be favoring all the wrong sorts of people. The peacemakers, the merciful, and those willing to endure persecution? These were not the expected first-round draft choices for a kingdom-building team! Many would have preferred vengeance over mercy, vindication over persecution, and fighting for freedom over making peace.

Consider a few other famous commands in the Sermon on the Mount, such as "love your enemy," "pray for those who persecute you," and the so-called "go the extra mile" (Mt. 5:41, 44). Sometimes these teachings are misunderstood as practical instructions for becoming pushovers for Jesus. But in their first-century context, these challenges would have been much more intense. In these commands, Jesus was subverting the revolutionary and nationalistic tendencies which pervaded much of first-century Judaism.

Take, for example, "love your enemy" (cf. Mt. 5:44). This was not simply an abstract principle to be applied when you had to face someone who wanted to do you harm. Rather this command had a specific, concrete meaning for the Jews who heard his teaching that day. For those original listeners, "love your enemy" could have sounded something like: "Love the Roman soldiers who killed your uncle when he was on pilgrimage to Jerusalem last year. Love Herod and his soldiers and tax collectors who took your land away from you."

Similarly, the command "if any one forces you to go one mile, go with him two miles" (Mt. 5:41) was not simply a lesson on being generous. Roman soldiers often forced civilians to carry their gear for one mile. Using this image, Jesus challenged the Jews to view the Romans not as adversaries to be overcome,

The peacemakers, the merciful? These were not the expected first-round draft choices for a kingdom-building team!

but as brothers and sisters who are to be loved and won over for God. If a Roman soldier from your town forces you to carry his belongings for one mile, love him and offer to carry it for a second mile.

In fact, that was Israel's mission from the very beginning: to be light to the world and salt of the earth (Mt. 5:13–14; Is. 42:6, 49:6). Jesus challenged the people to return to their roots and to be what Israel was always meant to be—not an exclusive, nationalistic religion isolated from the other nations, but a priestly kingdom serving the Gentiles and leading them to worship the one true God (cf. Ex. 19:5–6).

Israel was meant to be light to the world, God's instrument to bless the nations. But in the time of Jesus, many had lost sight of Israel's worldwide mission. Israel's light had turned inward on itself, focusing more on remaining ritually pure and separated from the pagans—as in the Pharisaic and Essene program—or intent on driving out the Romans with force, as in the revolt movements. How could Israel be light to the world if they were more concerned about running away from the world or fighting off the world?

Jesus shattered the prevailing views of the day with this challenge:

> You are the light of the world. A city set on a hill cannot be hid. Nor do men light a lamp and put it under a bushel, but on a stand, and it gives light to all in the house. Let your light so shine before men. (Mt. 5:14–16)

The way of the kingdom is the way of mission—mission to all the world, including sinners, gentiles and even the oppressors of the Jewish people. Sinners and tax collectors were not unclean people to run away from, but souls to reach with the call to repentance and the mercy of the kingdom. Similarly, Herod and the Romans were not enemies to be conquered, but brethren to be gathered back into God's covenant family.

TWO WAYS, TWO MOUNTAINS

Christ's challenge can be seen more clearly when we consider how Matthew's Gospel presents Jesus as a new Moses. Consider the many parallels: As infants, both Jesus and Moses escaped an evil ruler's decree to kill Israelite children by going to the Egyptians. Both came out of Egypt to return to Israel. Both went out into the desert in their adult years—Moses for forty years and Jesus for forty days. But the parallels between Jesus and Moses that are most significant for the Sermon on the Mount are found in what can be called "The Two Ways on the Two Mountains."

Just before Moses died, he challenged the people with a choice between *two ways* of life—two ways they could go when the entered the Promised Land—the way of faithfulness or unfaithfulness, life or death, blessing or curse:

> I have set before you life and death, blessing and curse; therefore choose life, that you and your descendants may live, loving the LORD your God, obeying his voice, and cleaving to him. (Deut. 30:19–20)

Moses gave instructions for these two ways of blessing and curse to be announced on *two mountains* after the people entered the land. Half the tribes of Israel shouted out the covenant blessings on Mount Ebal, while the other half proclaimed the curses on Mount Gerizim (Deut. 27:11–13). The Israelites had to choose which path they would follow. Faithfulness would bring blessing upon Israel as they dwelt in their land. Unfaithfulness would lead to the curses and expulsion from the land. The people chose the latter, and Jews many centuries later in the time of Jesus believed they were still suffering the consequences of their ancestors' sins as they suffered under foreign oppression just as Moses foretold.

All this background is crucial to understand Jesus' kingdom. Like Moses, Jesus offered the people two ways—the way of blessings and the way of curses. And he announced these two ways from two different mountains of his own. From the mountain in Galilee, he offered seven blessings known as "the Beatitudes" at the beginning of his ministry (Mt. 5:3–12). And on the Temple Mount in Jerusalem, he will announce seven curses to the scribes and the Pharisees who rejected him near the end of his ministry (Mt. 23:13–36).[1]

Two ways. Two Mountains. Blessings and Curses. Jesus' message is clear. Like Moses, Jesus was challenging the people of his day to make a choice: "Will you follow the way of separation like the Pharisees and Essenes? Or will you follow the way of loving your enemies and being light to the world? Do you want to follow the way of the revolutionaries? Or will

"Love your enemy" could have sounded something like: "Love the Roman soldiers who killed your uncle when he was visiting Jerusalem last year."

---

[1] Peter Ellis, *Matthew: His Mind and His Message* (Collegeville, MN: Liturgical Press, 1974), 81.

you follow the way of mercy, peace, and a willingness to endure persecution?" The first way will lead to Israel's destruction. The latter will lead to the kingdom's restoration. Ultimately Jesus will model for us how the true road to the kingdom is the way of the Cross.

Questions for Discussion

1. In what sense were the Jews facing a national crisis in the first century living under Roman rule? How did various movements within first-century Judaism respond to the crisis? Consider the following groups:

- Pharisees
- Essenes
- Revolutionaries

2. If you were a Jew in the time of Jesus, how would you have responded to this national crisis? Would you have followed the way of the Pharisees? The Essenes? The revolutionaries? How open do you think you might have been to Jesus' message and the type of kingdom he was initiating?

3. Read the Beatitudes in Matthew 5:3–12. How would these verses have been understood in their first-century Jewish context? Why would some of these blessings have been somewhat shocking to some Jews?

4. The teaching "You are the light of the world" is at the heart of Jesus' challenge for Israel in the Sermon on the Mount. In what ways is the Catholic Church called to live out Christ's challenge and be the "light of the world"? What specifically can we do to let our light shine more before all?

Chapter 6

Speaking Louder
than Words

IT HAS OFTEN BEEN SAID that "actions speak louder than words." This maxim is especially true for Jesus in the whirlwind of events following the famous Sermon on the Mount.

In this great sermon, Jesus challenged Israel to be "light to the world" and confronted the exclusive and nationalistic tendencies within the Judaism of his day.

However, while his words certainly left a deep impression on many, they were only a prelude to the more dramatic actions that followed when Jesus came down from that mountain. Matthew 8–9 records for us how Jesus immediately put his words into action. He performed ten miracles that shouted out a message that was much louder than anything he said in his sermon. Just as Moses "came down the mountain" at Sinai with the law, the Ten Commandments on stone, Jesus "came down the mountain" in Galilee with ten powerful actions that summed up the new law, his kingdom message in the Sermon on the Mount.

In remarkable fashion, Jesus cured a leper, healed a paralytic, restored sight to the blind, raised a child from the dead, and expelled demons. At the end of this *tour de force*, the crowds marveled, saying "Never was anything like this seen in Israel" (Mt. 9:33). But what was Jesus saying in these ten mighty deeds? Was Jesus trying to establish himself as some type of first-century faith healer? Did he perform these miracles simply to impress people or perhaps to prove his divinity? Looking at these powerful actions through the lens of first-century Judaism, we will see how practically every move Jesus made was charged with great symbolic meaning and played a key part in his plan of building his kingdom.

JESUS AND JOHN THE BAPTIST

John the Baptist had the same questions we do. He was wondering what the meaning was behind Jesus' mighty works. John heard about these miracles while he was in prison for having preached against the wicked deeds of King Herod. In this time of persecution and suffering, John's faith was tested, and he had some uncertainties about whether Jesus really was the Messiah. John might have been wondering, "If Jesus really is the Messi-

SPEAKING LOUDER THAN WORDS

ah-King, why am I still suffering here in prison? Why hasn't he freed me from Herod's terror?"

Wanting some reassurance from Jesus, John sent some of his own disciples to ask Jesus, "Are you he who is to come, or shall we look for another?" (Mt. 11:3). Jesus gave this answer to them:

> Go and tell John what you hear and see: the blind receive their sight and the lame walk, lepers are cleansed and the deaf hear, and the dead are raised up, and the poor have good news preached to them. (Mt. 11:4–5)

What kind of response was *that*? How would these words have answered John's important question? At first glance, Jesus does not seem to be very helpful. Instead of offering John the Baptist some reassurance and showing him some compassion, Jesus seems to be focused on himself and boasting about the amazing miracles he's performing.

Yet for those who know the Old Testament—as John the Baptist certainly did!—they would realize that Jesus was referring to a prophecy in Isaiah chapter 35 concerning the restoration of Israel:

> Behold, your God will come. . . . He will come and save you. Then the eyes of the blind shall be opened, and the ears of the deaf unstopped; then shall the lame man leap like a deer, and the tongue of the mute sing for joy. (Is. 35:4–6)

Jesus basically said to the disciples, "Go tell John what you have seen and heard—in other words, tell him that Isaiah 35 has come to fulfillment in me." That prophecy fulfillment certainly would have provided the reassurance John was seeking! It also offers us an insight into how Jesus interpreted his own miraculous healing and forgiving actions: They were not simply acts of kindness being bestowed on individuals needing God's help. They were that, but they were so much more. They were also public prophetic signs that God is now coming to rescue his people. Prophecy is being fulfilled. Israel is being restored. The long-awaited kingdom is finally here!

What is also significant is the type of people Jesus healed. Jews who suffered from leprosy and other illnesses would have been the outcasts in Jesus' day. They were excluded from society because they were ritually unclean. Only the pure and the physically whole were considered full Israelites.

This attitude was reflected in the writings of the Essenes. Consider the following fragment from an ancient Essene source (commonly called the Dead Sea Scrolls), which lists the type of people who were excluded from office in their community:

> No man smitten in his flesh,
> or paralysed in his feet or hands,
> or lame, or blind,
> or deaf, or dumb,
> or smitten in his flesh with a visible blemish. . .

none of these shall come to hold office among
the congregation.[1]

In this light, we see that Jesus' healing ministry went
far beyond curing bodily ailments. Jesus was bringing
these outsiders in. By healing them physically, he was
restoring them socially and religiously back into Israelite society. In this way, Jesus was symbolically showing
how all the traditional outcasts were among the first to
be included in his kingdom.

Let's look at the leper who knelt down before Jesus and begged him to make him clean (cf. Mt. 8:1–4).
Leprosy was one of the most dreaded diseases in ancient Judaism. Lepers were banished from society. They
were considered untouchables who had to announce
that they were coming by shouting out, "Unclean, unclean!" If a Jew touched a leper, he himself would become ritually unclean and would have to go through
ritual purification before being fit for Temple worship
again.

Yet when this particular leper asked Jesus to heal
him, Jesus did the unthinkable. He stretched out his
hand and touched the man! But something amazing
happened. Instead of becoming ritually defiled himself,
Jesus' holiness overpowered the uncleanness of the leper and the leper was cured. It was not Jesus who was
made unclean by touching the leper, but the leper was
made clean by touching Jesus!

---

[1] 1QSa2.5–9 in Geza Vermes, *The Dead Sea Scrolls in English* (New
York: Allen Lange The Penguin Press, 1997), 159.

In another episode, a woman suffering from a hemorrhage for twelve years desperately approached Jesus for healing. But she had to do so in a secretive way. With this ailment, the woman daily faced not only the physical danger of blood loss, but also the cultural shame of ritual uncleanness (cf. Lev. 15:25–30). She knew that any contact with Jesus would be considered as making him ritually unclean as well. Nevertheless, she said to herself, "If I only touch his garment, I shall be made well" and that's what she did. She came up from behind and touched the fringe of his garment in the hope of being cured (Mt. 9:21).

First-century Jews would have been shocked by such a bold action. They would have assumed that Jesus became defiled by coming into contact with her uncleanness. Once again, however, the opposite occurred. Instead of Jesus' becoming contaminated by her ritual impurity, the woman was healed instantly by the power of Jesus. Jesus had a healing power that far exceeded anything ever seen in the Old Testament. His holiness transformed the unholy. His cleanness wiped out the uncleanness. His sinlessness even purified sin.[2]

FORGIVING SINS

As his fame spread, crowds flocked to Jesus and begged him for help. The sick asked him for cures. Blind men cried out to him for sight. Even a Gentile official asked him to heal his servant.

---

[2] Curtis Mitch and Edward Sri, *The Gospel of Matthew* (Grand Rapids: Baker Academic, 2010), 126.

At the same time, Matthew tells the story of a paralyzed man who could not draw near to Jesus. His generous friends carried him to Jesus for help. Jesus, in turn, gave the man something much greater than anything he probably ever imagined. Not only did Jesus cure the man of his *physical* disability and give him the strength to stand up and walk, but Jesus also bestowed on him the power to walk again *spiritually* by forgiving his sins:

> And behold, they brought to him a paralytic, lying on his bed; and when Jesus saw their faith he said to the paralytic, "Take heart, my son; your sins are forgiven." (Mt. 9:2)

By forgiving this man's sins, Jesus deliberately engaged in an action that was extremely provocative. It shouted out good news, but in a way that might have alarmed some of those who witnessed this amazing event.

Forgiveness of sins surely was one of the chief signs of the New Covenant. Recall how the Jews interpreted their suffering under foreign domination as resulting from their own sinfulness (cf. Deut. 28:15–68; Dan. 9:1–19). That's why several prophecies from the Old Testament spoke of a New Covenant in which God would free Israel from their oppression and do so by freeing Israel from their sins (cf. Jer. 31:31–34; 33:4–11; Is. 43:25; Ezek. 36:25–27; Dan. 9:24). Forgiveness of sins and Israel's restoration went hand in hand. So when Jesus forgave sins, he was not simply bestowing private spiritual blessings on privileged individuals. Rather, he was announcing the fulfillment of everything the Jews were hoping for. By offering forgiveness of sins, Jesus was symbolically announcing the dawn of the New Covenant and the arrival of the long-awaited kingdom. Indeed, this was good news!

But not everyone took it that way. Instead of rejoicing, the scribes accused Jesus of blasphemy (Mt. 9:3). They believed that only God could forgive sins and he did so through the Temple priests and the Temple sacrifices. "Who does this man think he is, forgiving sins apart from the Temple?" they would ask.

Thus, in this simple action of saying "your sins are forgiven," Jesus claimed to do only what God could do. And he was saying to the Jews, "What you used to get at the Temple, in Jerusalem and through the Levitical priesthood you can get right here, right now, with me." In one broad stroke, Jesus bypassed the Temple system altogether and proclaimed himself the source of forgiveness of sins. Jesus made himself the new Temple, hinting that the days of the Temple in Jerusalem might be coming to an end. No wonder the scribes were so upset!

He was basically saying, "What you get at the Temple, you can get right here, right now, with me."

EATING WITH SINNERS

In addition to healing the sick and forgiving the sins of the people, Jesus was busy building his kingdom even while eating at the dinner table. Throughout his ministry, Jesus invited sinners and other outcasts of society to share a meal with him. This practice of open table fellowship, however, was much more than a gesture of warm hospitality. It was a subversive action which sparked much controversy. Consider this scene in Matthew 9:

> And as he sat at table in the house, behold, many tax collectors and sinners came and sat down with Jesus and his disciples. And when the Pharisees saw this, they said to his disciples, "Why does your teacher eat with tax collectors and sinners?" (Mt. 9:10–11)

Why were the Pharisees so upset? To understand their perspective, we need to know a little about the sacredness of meals in the first century.

We can't overestimate the importance of eating with "the right people" in first-century Judaism. In ancient Israel, meals were sacred. To invite someone to a meal was to practically invite them into your family.

In our modern society, we can sit down in a fast-food restaurant and have a meal alongside complete strangers and not think much about it. However, the ancient Israelites considered eating a meal with others a rather serious affair. Shared food and drink symbolized a shared life. They forged covenant bonds and were interpreted as establishing familial relationships—so much so that two enemies could seal a peace agreement by sharing a meal and then, afterwards, treat each other peacefully like family (cf. Gen. 26:26–31; 31:54–55). That's why the Jews generally ate only with extended family members or fellow Israelites of a similar social and religious class. Most loyal Jews never ate with gentiles or sinners.

More than any other group, the Pharisees gave special attention to table fellowship laws. In their desire to remain separate from anything or anyone unholy, the Pharisees taught that Jews should only eat with fellow Jews who were in good standing. In fact, 229 of their 341 laws dealt with table fellowship alone!

This helps explain why the Pharisees were so scandalized when Jesus ate with the sinners and tax collectors. How could Jesus sit at table with grave sinners who were ritually unclean and outside the covenant? How could he share a meal with the tax collectors—the traitors who collaborated with Rome and Herod and went around taking our money for the enemy?

Jesus seemed to be celebrating his kingdom with all the wrong people.

So when Jesus dined at table, he seemed to be celebrating his kingdom with all the wrong people. A true Jew would never think of doing such a thing!

In these eloquent actions, however, Jesus was making a bold statement. He deliberately chose these controversial dining partners to highlight the universality of his mission and to demonstrate his power to transform sinners and welcome them back into covenant fellowship.

Notice how Jesus responded to the Pharisees' complaint: "It is not the healthy who need the doctor, but the sick" (Mt. 9:12, *New Jerusalem Bible*)., *New Jerusalem Bible*). Just as a doctor must have contact with the sick, so does Jesus draw near to sinners to restore them to spiritual health. In this sense, his practice of eating with sinners and tax collectors signified a greater miracle than his healing of blindness, leprosy, and other illnesses. Without saying a word, Jesus symbolically restored these outcasts to God's covenant family and welcomed a surprise cast of members into the kingdom he was building.

Once again, his actions spoke louder than his words.

QUESTIONS FOR DISCUSSION

1. Jesus' healings were not only blessings for the individuals involved; they also sent a powerful symbolic message for the people of Israel as a whole. Read Isaiah 35:4–6. According to Isaiah, what will the signs be when God comes to save his people? Read Matthew 11:2–6. With the prophecy from Isaiah 35 in mind, how does Jesus' response answer John the Baptist's question? What is Jesus symbolically saying in his healing ministry?

2. Read Matthew 9:1–8. Here we learn that the paralyzed man has not only a physical ailment. He also has a spiritual problem that needs healing. He needs to be forgiven of his sins.

- What is the connection between sin and walking with God? How might sin make us unable to walk with God spiritually?
- What are some ways we can encounter Christ's forgiveness like the paralyzed man did that day?

3. Read Matthew 9:10–12. As we have seen, many pious Jews did not want to associate with non-Jews and other grave sinners. In what ways might faithful Christians today be tempted to fall into a similar trap?

4. While the Gospels never describe Jesus as associating with sinners in the midst of their sinful actions,

they do tell of Jesus constantly welcoming them and warmly inviting them into his table fellowship. How might Jesus' outreach to sinners serve as a model for the Christian's relationship with unbelievers and those who may not be living out their Christian life? Specifically, how can you challenge yourself to extend fellowship to those who might not share the same values, interests, and ideas as you do? How might such fellowship help lead others to a deeper relationship with Jesus and the Catholic Church?

5. Consider the story of the hemorrhaging woman touching Jesus' garment (Matthew 9:20-22). Put yourself in her shoes. Consider some burden that you carry—some wound, hurt, fear, weakness or sin. How might her story encourage you?

- What are some ways we can reach out and seek Christ to help us with our burdens in life today?

Chapter 7

Conflict in Galilee

MATTHEW 10–12

BY THE END OF CHAPTER NINE in Saint Matthew's Gospel, we see that Jesus has captivated everyone's attention and has won the hearts of the people. All of Israel is excited about Jesus' kingdom movement . . . or so it appears at first glance.

We know that Jesus attracted large crowds from all over Palestine. Many traveled great distances to witness firsthand the exciting movement he was starting in Galilee (cf. Mt. 4:24–25). Just when his fame was reaching its peak, Jesus took the opportunity to lead large crowds of followers into the Galilean hillside to issue a startling summons which today is referred to as "the Sermon on the Mount" (Mt. 5–7). In this famous discourse, Jesus set forth his kingdom agenda, and the crowds marveled at his words, recognizing him as an authoritative teacher from God (cf. Mt. 7:28–29).

Then Jesus came down from that mountain to perform ten miracles, which drew even more fanfare. He cleansed lepers, calmed storms, and cured the sick. He healed a crippled man, forgave sins, and restored sight to the blind. However, these mighty actions in Galilee did not reach their climax until Jesus performed his tenth and greatest miracle of all: expelling a demon from a mute man (cf. Mt. 9:32–34).

Why might an exorcism be considered his greatest miracle so far? In today's world, we do not often hear about exorcisms, let alone see them performed in the middle of our city streets. Yet for a first-century Jew, Jesus' driving out evil spirits would have been much more than just another exciting miracle.

When Jesus commanded a demon to leave an individual, he was not simply offering spiritual freedom to that particular person. Rather, his exorcisms sent a message that had great meaning for *all* the people of Israel: Jesus was fighting Israel's most important battle. He was building God's kingdom by driving out those demonic forces which had attacked the Israelite nation since the beginning of their history.

By expelling demons, Jesus boldly proclaimed his supreme authority as the Messiah-King. Although his other miraculous healings demonstrated his power over things of this world—such as diseases, physical ailments, and the skies and seas—Jesus' exorcisms showed that he had authority even over the spiritual realm. By issuing commands over the demons, Jesus manifested his power over the devil himself—the source of all evils in this world.

Such actions, indeed, stirred up hopes for the Messiah. In Jewish tradition, David's son, King Solomon, was known for his exorcisms and power over demons.[1] That's why some people responded to Jesus' exorcisms by saying, "Can this be the Son of David?" (Mt. 12:23). And since the Jews expected the Messiah to be a descendent of David who would fight Israel's enemies, Jesus' mighty power over the greatest enemy, Satan, could have been interpreted as a messianic action.

So Jesus culminated his initial, incredible tour of miraculous works in Galilee by expelling the demon from the mute man (cf. Mt. 9:32–33). This final climactic act captivated the crowds and left them completely astonished. They marveled at his ministry, saying "Never was anything like this seen in Israel" (Mt. 9:33). Jesus seems to have had the crowd in the palms of his hands.

Not everyone, however, was so impressed.

A SEVERE ACCUSATION

Just when Jesus' movement seemed to be taking off with immense popularity, the Pharisees conspired to drag him down and bring an end to all the commotion his miracles had caused. They did not like what they were seeing in Galilee. Jesus claimed to be announcing the long-awaited kingdom that God had promised Israel, but he seemed to be establishing it in all the

---

[1] See Wisdom 7:17–20. See also the pseudepigraphic Testament of Solomon for an example of one strand of this tradition in Judaism in *The Old Testament Pseudepigigrapha*, vol. 1, James H. Charlesworth, ed. (New York: Doubleday, 1983), 960–87.

wrong ways and inviting all the wrong people. Sinners, prostitutes, and tax collectors were drawn into his table fellowship. He touched lepers and the diseased and spent time with other "untouchables." He even claimed to offer forgiveness of sins on his own authority apart from the established priesthood and the Temple system. "Who does this man think he is?" they would have asked themselves. Surely, he could not have been from God. In their eyes, Jesus must have been a "false prophet" since he was seemingly leading the people astray in so many serious matters.

Yet the Pharisees could not deny Jesus' miraculous works. Everyone agreed that something supernatural was going on in Jesus' ministry. His works were so great that they must have been based on some higher spiritual power. The crowds attributed his mighty works to the power of God, but the Pharisees saw things rather differently. Since Jesus seemed to be leading the people away from God's Temple and the priesthood, and since he seemed to be associating with all who were unclean, the Pharisees concluded that Jesus could not have been a man sent by God. So if Jesus is performing miracles and even expelling demons, he must not be doing it by God's power, but by using a much darker force: "He casts out demons by the prince of demons," they said (Mt. 9:34).

> *The Pharisees weren't merely saying they disagreed with Jesus. They were accusing Jesus of being Satanic.*

Let's feel the weight of that accusation. The Pharisees weren't merely saying they disagreed with Jesus or disliked his ministry. They didn't accuse Jesus of teaching false doctrine or committing a great sin. *They were accusing Jesus of being Satanic.* That's quite a severe charge! They were arguing that the only reason Jesus could issue commands over the demons was because he himself was in league with the prince of demons, Satan.

This was a clear sign of the Pharisees' quickly growing hostility toward Jesus. After this, they put him under surveillance, watching every move he made, trying to find any small grounds on which they could criticize him. They tried to trap him in his own words. They even began plotting how to destroy him (Mt. 12:14). The conflict escalated when Jesus expelled a demon from another man in Galilee. Once again, the people were amazed, but the Pharisees leveled a serious charge against Jesus: "It is only by Beelzebul, the prince of demons, that this man casts out demons" (Mt. 12:24).

The Pharisees had gone one step too far. Jesus shows them the severity of their accusation:

> But if it is by the Spirit of God that I cast out demons, then the kingdom of God has come upon you. . . [E]very sin and blasphemy will be forgiven men, but the blasphemy against the Spirit will not be forgiven. (Mt. 12:28, 31)

In other words, the Pharisees were blaspheming against God's own Spirit. If Jesus expelled demons by the power of the Holy Spirit, then the Pharisees were identifying that Holy Spirit of Jesus with the power of the devil. That is serious blasphemy. Jesus wants to forgive everyone. But if the Pharisees cut themselves off from the very source of salvation—Jesus and his Spirit—there was nothing more Jesus could do to work with them. It is in this sense that this particular sin cannot be forgiven. They had closed themselves off from the very Spirit by which Jesus offered forgiveness of sins.

THE NEW ISRAEL

Jesus knew that Israel needed a drastic change in spiritual leadership. He looked upon the crowds with great sadness, knowing that their own leaders would steer them away from him.

> When he saw the crowds, he had compassion for them, because they were harassed and helpless, like sheep without a shepherd. Then he said to his disciples, "The harvest is plentiful, but the laborers are few; pray therefore the Lord of the harvest to send out laborers into his harvest." (Mt. 9:36–38)

At this point in the ministry, Jesus did something he had not done before. After seeing that the people of Israel were like sheep without a shepherd and in desperate need of new leaders to guide them, Jesus turned to his close followers and singled out twelve men to be special leaders in his kingdom. This choosing of the twelve apostles marked a major shift in the ministry of Jesus.

For the Jewish people, the number twelve was much more than a dozen. This sacred number brought to mind the twelve tribes of Israel which descended from the patriarch Jacob's twelve sons. These twelve tribes were the foundation stones upon which the nation of Israel had been built. Jesus drew upon this traditional symbolism. By going among his numerous followers and pulling twelve men aside to be his close associates, Jesus was sending an important message. Without saying a word, this action of choosing *twelve* men for special duty would have said, "The New Israel is here with me and these twelve men!" This action alone could have signaled that all the Jewish hopes for a renewed Israel were coming to fulfillment in Jesus' movement.

Therefore, when Jesus chooses *twelve* apostles, he's symbolically expressing his intention to rebuild Israel—to reconstitute Israel around himself with the apostles as the central leaders.

BUILDING THE CHURCH

The word "apostle" means "one who is sent." An apostle represents the one who sends him, and shares in that person's authority. Matthew's Gospel draws our attention to this important point by an intricate display of literary art. Using a technique called "chiasm," Matthew draws a number of parallels between what Jesus does in 9:35–38 and the mission he gives the apostles in 10:1–8. Jesus *preaches the kingdom and heals the sick* (9:35), and he sees the people are like *sheep without a shepherd* (9:36) and in need for God to "*send out*" laborers to them (9:38). To address this need, Jesus chooses "*the twelve*" apostles (9:38).

All of this parallels exactly in reverse order what comes next in Matthew's narrative. Matthew lists the names of "*the twelve*" apostles (10:2) and *sends out* those apostles (10:5) as shepherds to the "*lost sheep*" of the house of Israel (10:5) so that they may *preach the Gospel of the kingdom and heal the sick* just as Jesus did (10:7–8).

In a chiasm's structure, what is most important is what is in the middle of all the parallels. That's what the narrator is trying to emphasize. At the center of these parallels in Matthew 9–10 is Jesus' choosing twelve apostles and *giving them authority* (10:1–2).

The theme of Jesus' authority is important for Matthew. In the opening chapter, he demonstrates Jesus' messianic authority as a true Son of David with his royal lineage traced in the genealogy. Matthew 2 emphasizes Jesus's authority in his fulfilling many ancient Jewish prophecies. Matthew 3 shows Jesus' authority as the anointed King when the Spirit descends upon him at the Jordan River. In Matthew 4, Jesus exercises his authority over the devil, defeating him in the three desert temptations. In Matthew 5–7, Jesus establishes his authority in his teachings in the Sermon on the Mount as the people recognize he teaches with authority (7:29), and in Matthew 8–9 he manifests his authority over the storms, the sea, disease, infirmities, and even demonic spirits. Matthew 1–9 is all about demonstrating Jesus' messianic authority through his words and deeds.

But in Matthew 10, *that very authority of Jesus is*

When Jesus chooses twelve apostles, he's symbolically expressing his intention to rebuild Israel.

88

now being shared with the twelve apostles. After the Pharisees accused Jesus of working with Satan (9:34), Jesus summoned the twelve apostles to be the leaders of the renewed Israel he was building.

Apostolic Authority

Matthew 9:35–10:8

A. Jesus went about *preaching* the Gospel of *the kingdom* and *healing* (9:35)

  B. The people are like "*sheep without a shepherd*" (9:36)

   C. Pray the Lord to *send out* laborers (9:38)

    D. Jesus called *the twelve* disciples (10:1)

     E. Jesus gave the twelve authority (10:1)

    D'. The names of "*the twelve*" (10:2)

   C'. Jesus *sent out* the twelve (10:5)

  B'. Jesus sent them to "the *lost sheep* of the house of Israel" (10:6)

A'. Apostles *preached* "*the kingdom* of heaven is at hand" and *healed* (10:7–8)

To emphasize the reality of the apostle's authority, Jesus went on to say to them, "He who receives you receives me" (Mt. 10:40). Invested with the authority of Jesus himself, the apostles' role as representatives of Jesus is very clear: If you wanted to accept him, you had to accept his apostles.

Imagine what would happen if someone said to Jesus, "I want a relationship with just you, not your apostles. . . . I like you, but I can't stand Peter. . . . I'm willing to follow you, Jesus, but I can't accept the leadership of James and John"? Jesus would say that whoever receives his apostles receives him. In fact, Luke's Gospel incorporates another teaching of Jesus on this point. Jesus also says to the apostles, "Whoever receives you, receives me. And whoever rejects you rejects me" (Luke 10:16). That's how closely Jesus associates himself with his twelve apostles!

This is why we today are called to accept the shepherding of the modern-day apostles, the bishops, who stand as the successors of the original twelve (cf. CCC 861–62). By receiving their guidance and teaching, we allow the Good Shepherd himself to guide our lives through his representatives here on earth. Consider the prayer that priests recite in Masses for Feasts of the Apostles:

> You are the eternal Shepherd
> who never leaves his flock untended.
> Through the apostles
> you watch over us and protect us always.
> You made them shepherds of the flock
> to share in the work of your Son. . . .[2]

---

[2] As found in CCC 857.

QUESTIONS FOR DISCUSSION

1. Jesus' exorcisms are the most powerful display of his power—showing his power even over the devil. Read Matthew 9:32–34 and 12:22–24. How do the crowds respond to Jesus' exorcisms? How do the Pharisees respond?

2. Read Matthew 12:25–32. Why does Jesus consider the Pharisees' accusation a blasphemy against the Holy Spirit? In what sense does Jesus say this sin is unforgivable? Is it too big of a sin for Jesus to forgive?

3. Read Matthew 9:36–38. What does Jesus say about the leaders ("shepherds") of the Jewish people?

4. Jesus chose twelve apostles and gave them authority to preach the Gospel of the Kingdom and heal every disease and infirmity (Mathew 10:1–8). Read Matthew 9:34; 9:36-38.Why does he choose the twelve at this point in his ministry? What is the symbolism of Jesus' choosing twelve apostles?

5. In light of Matthew 10, especially 10:40, how would you respond to the following comment: "I just want to follow Jesus. I don't need a Church or any bishops. Jesus is my Good Shepherd; he will lead me. I'm spiritual but not religious. I love Jesus but don't need a Church"?

Chapter 8

The Surprise of
the Parables

HAVE YOU EVER considered how *shocking* Jesus' parables
must have been to his original audience in Galilee?

At a crucial turning point in his ministry, Jesus dramatically shifts his teaching method. After several cit-
ies don't accept his message, after the Pharisees accuse
him of being Satanic and after they start plotting how
to destroy him, Jesus, all of a sudden, begins to teach
the people "many things in parables" (Mt. 13:3).

This marks the first time Matthew uses the word
"parable." While Jesus had used some parable-like teaching before, this is the first time he issues a whole series of
parables, one after another in rapid-fire succession. "All
this Jesus said to the crowds in parables; indeed he said

nothing to them without a parable" (Mt. 13:34).

His disciples notice the dramatic change in approach. This was not normal. They are very surprised. "Then the disciples came and said to him, "Why do you speak to them in parables?" (Mt. 13:10).

It is sometimes said that Jesus taught in parables in order to make his message easy for more people to understand. He used simple images from daily life to make his complex teachings more accessible to the simple folk he was addressing.

But is that really the case? In the Jewish biblical tradition, parables were not about "dumbing down" a complicated message. Rather, parables were cryptic sayings that were meant to stimulate thought. They came in the form of short riddles, proverbs, and allegories. Parables also appeared as stories which challenged listeners to enter into the plot and ponder its deeper meaning—to think about how the different characters in the story act and what implications that might have for their own lives.

Sometimes parables were even told to condemn corrupt leaders and stir them to repent of their sins (Is. 5:1–7; Ezek. 17:2–21; 19:2–19). Consider one of the most famous parables in the Old Testament: the parable the prophet Nathan told to confront King David with his sins (2 Sam. 12:1–10).

David had committed adultery with a woman named Bathsheba. He tried to cover up his sin by having her husband, Uriah—who was a soldier in David's army—killed. David ordered Uriah to be put in the front line of battle at the moment the rest of the troops would retreat. Few people knew about David's adultery and murder. But God knew. And he sent the prophet Nathan to confront David with his sin.

One can imagine the trepidation Nathan would have had about this mission. David just murdered someone in order to keep his sin secret. And now Nathan is commanded by God to go to David and bring the whole affair out in the open? Will David kill Nathan, too, in order to keep his sin from going public?

Nathan wisely doesn't bring up the topic directly with David. He instead tells the king a parable. He tells of a rich man who had many flocks of sheep and a poor man who had only one ewe lamb. One day, the rich man stole the poor man's only lamb and cooked it for a guest he was hosting. Upon hearing *Sometimes parables were told to condemn corrupt leaders and stir them to repent.* this story, David was outraged and said, "As the LORD lives, the man who has done this deserves to die." At this, Nathan famously replies to David, "You are the man" (2 Sam. 12:5–7).

Indeed, David is like the rich man in the story. David, who had multiple wives of his own, took the poor man Uriah's only wife for himself and had Uriah killed on the battlefield.

But there's more. Nathan doesn't just tell any story about the powerful exploiting the weak. He specifically tells a story about sheep. Why? Because David himself had been a noble shepherd. David grew up caring for his sheep, risking his own life to fight off lions and bears to protect his flock (1 Sam. 17:34–35). Sheep were very dear to David. So when David hears a story about a wealthy man stealing a poor man's one ewe lamb, this isn't any ordinary story of injustice. This is exactly the kind of story to which David would relate most personally. From his own experience of caring for his sheep, David would deeply feel the weight of the rich man's wicked deed.

That's why David responds so passionately, condemning this man to death. And it's at that very moment, when David feels the rich man's sin the most, that Nathan reveals how David himself is like the wicked man in the story.

Nathan's parable works. David is so emotionally invested in the story that his heart is pierced when he suddenly realizes he himself is like the "bad guy" in the plot. David doesn't get mad at Nathan. He doesn't get defensive. He doesn't even try to make excuses for himself. The parable pierced through his hard heart and David melted. He humbly admits his horrible sins and repents (2 Sam. 12:13; cf. Ps. 51).

That's what parables sometimes do. They shake people up. They get people who are set in their ways to consider a different way of looking at things. They draw the listener into the story, but at the end, there's a surprising twist and the listener is left wondering what the significance is—Is that about me? Where do I fit in the story? Am I like the villain in the plot?

THE SECRETS OF THE KINGDOM

This background sheds light on what Jesus himself says

about his own parables. When his disciples ask him why he starts to teach the crowds in parables, Jesus answers,

> To you it has been given to know the secrets of the kingdom of heaven, but to them it has not been given. For to him who has will more be given, and he will have abundance; but from him who has not, even what he has will be taken away. (Mt. 13:11–12)

What does *that* mean? This doesn't sound like a simplification of Jesus' message so that more people can understand. It seems like just the opposite. Jesus says *less* people will be given deeper understanding. Jesus is letting his disciples in on the secrets of the kingdom, but not the crowds.

Those who are receptive to Christ's teaching will receive more understanding. But for those who have closed hearts, the little understanding they have will now be taken away. They'll receive less straightforward teaching from Jesus and now be forced to ponder the deeper significance of his more cryptic parables.

Only the receptive ones—the disciples—will get from Jesus the explanations of the parables. Jesus, in fact, takes the disciples aside and unpacks the meaning for them (Mt. 13:10–23; 36–43). But there are many people in Capernaum and the surrounding areas who have seen and heard a lot in Christ's ministry. They have *heard* his teachings and have *seen* his many miracles, but have not responded to the kingdom and repented. Their hearts are closed, so they will not get the deeper explanation of the parables. Jesus himself explains, "This is why I speak to them in parables, because *seeing* they do not see, and *hearing* they do not hear, nor do they understand" (Mt.13:13).

Let's see how this works in the first and foundational parable Jesus tells this day, the "Parable of the Sower." Here, Jesus draws

That's what parables sometimes do. They shake people up.

not only on a common agricultural image but a familiar Old Testament symbol. In the Jewish Scriptures, God is likened to a sower and his seed represents God's Word (Is. 55:10–13). Jesus picks up the image and applies it to himself. He is the sower and the seed is his teaching as he proclaims his kingdom in Galilee.

He tells how the sower goes out to sow his seed. Some seeds fall on bad soil—on a *path* where birds come to eat it, on *rock* where it couldn't grow roots, and amid *thorns* that choke it. Other seeds fall on good soil and bear much fruit.

This passage is commonly interpreted as a spiritual story for all ages about being faithful, receiving God's word in our lives and bearing fruit in the world. It also had a specific significance for the original hearers at this precise moment in Jesus' ministry. Jesus is the sower sowing the seeds of his teachings as he proclaims the kingdom in Galilee. And the path, rocky ground, thorns and good soil represent the various kinds of responses the people in Galilee had to his ministry. The original audience consisting of the crowds, the Pharisees and others are left wondering what this parable means and how it might apply to them: what kind of soil have they been in receiving the seed of Christ's teachings?

But Jesus gives the deeper explanation of this parable to his disciples (Mt. 13:18–23). He tells them that some people hear the word of the kingdom but do not understand it (Mt. 13:19). Who might this describe? Which group in Jesus' public ministry has heard Christ's words proclaiming the kingdom but have misunderstood it? This sounds a lot like the Pharisees who have mistaken Christ's kingdom for being in league with Satan and who are plotting to destroy him (Mt. 12:14, 24). They are like the seed that falls on the path and the enemy snatches the seed away.

Jesus also explains to his disciples that there are others who receive his teachings with joy, at least at first (Mt. 13:20–21). But when faced with persecution, they fall away. Who in Matthew's Gospel so far fits this description? The crowds. Initially, they respond enthusiastically to Christ's Sermon on the Mount (Mt. 7:28) and to his many miracles, saying, "Never was anything like this seen in all of Israel" (Mt. 9:33). But the crowd's enthusiasm will be nowhere to be found on Good Friday. The crowds on that day will shout out "Crucify him! Crucify him!" People who are merely impressed by dynamic preaching and wondrous miracles but don't allow God's Word to take deep root in their lives are not likely to persevere in faith. They are like the seeds that fall on rocky ground— they spring up rapidly at the first, but they have no root. Jesus explains what will happen to such a person: "when tribulation or persecution arises on account of the word, immediately he falls away" (Mt. 13:21).

Jesus also tells his disciples that there are some who hear God's word, but "the cares of the world and the delight in riches choke the word" (Mt. 13:22). This description recalls how Jesus warned his disciples and others to put the kingdom first and not to be anxious over the concerns of this world (Mt. 6:25–34; 8:18–24). It also may foreshadow the "rich young man" who wanted to follow Christ but turned away from discipleship because he had too many possessions (Mt. 19:16–22). These are like the seed that falls amid the thorns. The seed starts to grow but is choked by the person's attachments to the riches and cares of this world.

Finally, Jesus explains that there are some who hear the word and understand it. They will bear much fruit (Mt. 13:23). This, of course, points to the disciples themselves who have been open to Christ's teachings and have made many sacrifices to follow Jesus. They will bear much fruit for the kingdom.

THE SAME DAY

It's important to notice the context in which Jesus suddenly broke out with these eight parables. This shift took place "on the same day" the Pharisees accused Jesus of being in league with Satan and Jesus confronted them on their blasphemy (Mt. 12:22–50; 13:1). These eight parables also come on the heels of the Pharisees starting to plot his death (Mt. 12:14) and the many people in Galilee who had seen his signs and wonders but still refused to repent (Mt. 11:20–24).

All this is crucial background for understanding the parables given that day: In some of these parables, Jesus contrasts good and bad soil, wheat and weeds, and good fish and bad fish (Mt. 13:3–9, 24–30, 47–50). These contrasts point to the varied responses to his kingdom, some people welcoming it and others rejecting it.

Other parables that day highlight the exemplary response to the kingdom which his disciples have exhibited. A true disciple is like a man selling all he has for a pearl of great price or a hidden treasure (Mt. 13:44–45). Indeed, his disciples are like this. They have given up everything to follow Christ like the men in these parables.

Still other parables simply shed light on the mystery of the kingdom's littleness. Some might wonder, "How can Christ's small movement of only a few faithful followers really be the Kingdom of Heaven? If Jesus is the messiah, why isn't there a much larger following?" Jesus explains that his kingdom is not a political, military or economic powerhouse. Rather, it's like a tiny mustard seed that will grow into a large bush. It's like a small amount of yeast that will leaven a whole batch of flour (Mt. 13:31–33). Indeed, this small band of faithful disciples might not be impressive by the world's standards, but it will grow, expand, and multiply over time.

Eventually, the whole world will be changed through them and their successors—especially the one to whom Jesus is about to give the keys of the kingdom.

Questions for Discussion

1. How were parables often used in the Old Testament (2 Samuel 12:1-10; Isaiah 5:1–7; Ezekiel 17:2–21; 19:2–19)? How might this background shed light on Jesus' use of parables? How might this background have changed the way you think about Jesus' parables?

2. Why does Jesus begin to speak to the people in parables? What just happened that made him change his teaching method?

3. In the Parable of the Sower, Jesus warns that there are some who initially receive God's Word with joy but fall away when persecution comes because the seed does not take root. What can we do to have our faith take deeper root in our life?

4. In the Parable of the Sower, Jesus warns that there are some who hear God's Word, but "the cares of the world and the delight in riches choke the word" (13:22). What concerns of the world sometimes hinder the life of the Christian? In what ways might our interest in the comforts and riches of this world begin to choke our faith life?

Chapter 9

The Keys to the Kingdom

IF YOU EVER HAVE THE CHANCE to visit the Vatican, go to the center of St. Peter's Basilica and just look up. You can't miss it. Some of the most important words Jesus ever spoke will stare down at you. Encircling the base of the dome, a line of six-foot-tall black letters pressed onto a gold background majestically spell out in Latin: *"You are Peter, and on this rock I will build my Church, and I will give you the keys of the kingdom of heaven."*

Even after visiting St. Peter's countless times during my years of study in Rome, I am still moved whenever I see these sacred words spoken to Peter some two thousand years ago. They not only mark a crucial turning point in Jesus' kingdom movement, but they are also commonly hailed as an important foundation for the role of the pope in Christ's kingdom today. Imagine what it would have been like to have been there during that pivotal conversation between Jesus and Peter. Let us go back to Caesarea Philippi, where these words were spoken for the first time, so that we may hear them anew in the way the twelve apostles themselves might have originally understood them.

Most of Matthew's Gospel so far has been focused on Jesus' ministry in the northern region of Israel known as Galilee. But in Matthew 16, his kingdom program takes a significant turn. Jesus leads his twelve apostles north to the district known as Caesarea Philippi—one of the northernmost points in his public ministry. There, he initiated a conversation that would forever leave its mark on Christian history.

Jesus began by asking the apostles about the public's perception of him and his ministry. What were the people saying about him? The apostles reported that some thought Jesus was John the Baptist, while others thought he was Elijah, Jeremiah, or another one of the prophets. After hearing about what the crowds were saying, Jesus then turned to the twelve and posed the question on a more personal level: "But who do *you* say that I am?" (Mt. 16:15).

At this, Simon Peter took the lead and answered for them all: "You are the Christ, the Son of the living God" (Mt. 16:16). In other words, Peter was saying, "You are the anointed king we have been longing for. You are the one who will restore Israel and set us free." With these words, Peter became the first person in

Matthew's Gospel explicitly to recognize Jesus as the long-awaited Messiah.

Jesus then responded to Peter's insight by blessing him and saying:

> Blessed are you, Simon Bar-Jona! For flesh and blood has not revealed this to you, but my Father who is in heaven. And I tell you, you are Peter, and on this rock I will build my church, and the powers of death shall not prevail against it. I will give you the keys of the kingdom of heaven, and whatever you bind on earth shall be bound in heaven, and whatever you loose on earth shall be loosed in heaven. (Mt. 16:17–19)

These famous words serve as the foundation for understanding the role of the pope in the life of the Catholic Church. Yet, some may object that the passage doesn't appear to say anything about Peter's being an authoritative head of the Church and the Vicar of Christ, much less about his having successors who would continue this role of shepherding all Christians. Indeed, at first glance, some might say Jesus doesn't seem to be intending to start any type of ongoing papal lineage at all!

However, when we read these words through the lenses of first-century Judaism, we see just how significant these words would have been for Jesus and how profoundly they might shed light on the unique leadership role he gave Peter and Peter's successors throughout the centuries down to today.

A NEW NAME

The first thing about Jesus' words to Peter which would have captured the apostles' attention is the fact that Jesus changed Simon's name. This was not about giving Simon a new nickname. In Jewish tradition, a change in someone's name signified a change in the person. When God set certain people apart for special roles, he sometimes gave them new names to signify their new purpose in the divine plan. For example, Abram's name is changed to Abraham (which means "father of a multitude") when Yahweh chose him to become the "father of a multitude of nations" (Gen. 17:5). Similarly, the patriarch Jacob's name was changed to Israel as he was being prepared to become the father of the twelve tribes of the nation of Israel.

A new name signals a new mission. Thus, when Jesus gave Simon a new name, he was setting him apart from the other twelve apostles and bestowing on him a special function. This simple name change alone would have signaled to those apostles and first-century Jews that Jesus was giving Peter an important role to play in his kingdom.

The second element that would have stood out in Jesus' words to Peter would have been the new name itself. Jesus conferred on Simon the name *"Peter"—Kepha* in Jesus' language (Aramaic)—which means "rock." What is interesting is that *Kepha* was not commonly used as a proper name at that time. Although Peter is a common name found in many modern languages today, this was not the case in Jesus' day. Jesus took an ordinary word—rock—and used it to designate a human being, Simon Peter. The peculiarity of such an action would be similar to having your name changed to a word such as "mountain" or some other word that is not normally used as a proper name.

What did Jesus mean when he called Simon by this non-name, "rock"? And what did he mean when he told him he would build his Church on him and the gates of death would not prevail against it?

A number of images come to mind. On a basic level, Jesus was simply saying that Peter will be rock-like: a durable, solid foundation giving the Church the firm and stable leadership it will need in the years ahead. Indeed, the apostles may have thought of a famous, massive rock structure found at Caesarea Philippi since they were near there. On another level, Peter will be like Abraham who was described as the rock on which God constructed and established the world (cf. Is. 51:1–2). These allusions point to the pivotal role Peter would play in God's plan for the Church.

But there is another significant image Jesus probably was thinking of most when he gave Simon the name "rock"—the most important rock in all of Judaism: the "foundation stone" (Heb. *eben shetiyah*) in the Jerusalem Temple.

According to Jewish tradition, the foundation stone served not only as the base of the altar for sacrifice in the Temple. In ancient Jewish lore, this rock also was associated with significant moments of salvation history. The foundation stone was believed to be originally the site of creation and the foundation on which God built the world. It was the place where Noah's ark found rest after the flood and where Abraham was willing to sacrifice his son Isaac to Yahweh. David dug down to this rock and made it the foundation for the Temple. And it was believed that this rock plugged up the waters of the abyss, the pit of death, and kept the demonic forces of deception and death sealed down below.[1]

These were vivid images that the Jews used to describe the profound reality of the Temple's relationship with the spiritual order. Simply put, the Temple was the sacred space where heaven and earth met. For the ancient Jews, the Temple was the center of the universe, and the foundation stone was the point of intersection between the spiritual realm and the physical world.

Whatever one may make of these ancient Jewish traditions, what is important for us to note is how Jesus used similar images when he referred to Simon as the *rock* upon which he would build his Church, and *the gates of death would not prevail against it*. In other words, Jesus seems to be saying that Peter is like the Temple foundation stone. Just as God used the Temple rock to build the world and protect it from the chaotic waters and evil spirits underneath, so too God will use Peter to build the Church and protect his people from the powers of death.[2]

---

[1] Thomas Fawcett, *Hebrew Myth and Christian Gospel* (London: SCM, 1973), 239–45; Zev Vilnay, *Legends of Jerusalem* (Philadelphia: Jewish Publication Society of America, 1973), 5–82; Roland de Vaux, *Ancient Israel* (New York: McGraw-Hill, 1965), 318–19; cf. Rev. 20.

[2] Fawcett, *Hebrew Myth*, 244–45; de Vaux, *Ancient Israel*, 318–19.

KEYS TO THE KINGDOM

After changing Simon's name to Peter, Jesus did something else that made Peter's important position in the kingdom even more obvious. He gave Peter "the keys of the kingdom":

> I will give you the keys of the kingdom of heaven, and whatever you bind on earth shall be bound in heaven, and whatever you loose on earth shall be loosed in heaven. (Mt. 16:19)

What is the significance of "the keys of the kingdom" Jesus gives to Peter? Here, Jesus is drawing upon an important symbol in the Old Testament Scriptures—the keys of the Davidic Kingdom. And those keys pointed to a crucial leadership position in the Kingdom of Judah—the "head of the household" or "master of the palace"—which was the king's highest ranking official in the royal court.

Similar to prime minister-like positions in other ancient near-eastern kingdoms, the master of the palace in the Davidic dynasty shared in the king's own authority, governed in the king's name, and acted for him in his absence.[3] His role took on the greatest importance when the king was away, for example, on a diplomatic mission or military campaign.

Isaiah 22 describes the promotion of a man named Eliakim to this most prestigious office. As master of

---

[3] De Vaux, *Ancient Israel*, 130.

the palace, Eliakim handled the day-to-day affairs of
the kingdom for the king. He wore a royal robe and
exercised authority, ruling as a father figure over the
people of Judah. This new
master of the palace was
described as "a peg in a sure
place" and "a throne of hon-
or" to his father's house (Is.
22:15–25). To symbolize the
unique authority bestowed upon him, the master of the
palace was given *the key of the house of David.*

*Jesus was probably thinking
of the most important rock in
Judaism: the "foundation stone"
in the Jerusalem Temple.*

This is the royal imagery Jesus was alluding to
when he gave Peter the keys to the kingdom. Jesus
was saying that Peter will be the new "master of the
palace" in the kingdom he was building. Since the keys
symbolized how the Davidic king vested the prime
minister with his very authority, Jesus was saying a
lot when he gave Peter the keys to the kingdom. It
was as if he was saying: "I am the anointed King—the
Christ, Messiah. You, Peter, will be the prime minister
in my kingdom. You will be in charge of the day-to-
day affairs of my kingdom. You will be vested with my
very authority so that you can shepherd the people in
my name."

SUCCESSION

Up to this point, we have seen that Jesus certainly singled out Peter for having a unique role in his kingdom. Peter underwent a name change signifying his
special vocation. He was the foundation rock for the

Church, keeping even the powers of evil at bay. And he was given the keys to the kingdom, designating him as the prime minister, ruling with Jesus' authority in the Church. Matthew's Gospel clearly shows us that Peter was elevated to a preeminent position of authority in Christ's kingdom.

But where do Catholics get the idea of an ongoing papacy, a line of successors serving in this role *after* Peter? Some might argue that all we can conclude from the passage is that *Peter* was given this special authoritative position. It is one thing to say that Jesus established Peter as the head of the Church, but it is another thing to claim that Jesus intended for there to be successors to Peter's office throughout the centuries down to the present pope today. Where does Matthew 16 mention anything about Peter's special authority being *passed on to successors?*

The answer again lies in the keys. The role of the master of the palace was not a one-time appointed position. It was an office. When one person stepped out of the role, another would step in as the successor. That's the whole context of Isaiah 22, which tells how Eliakim was replacing the previous master of the palace, a man named Shebna. To symbolize the transfer of the office from Shebna to Eliakim, Eliakim was given the key to the house of David (cf. Is. 22:22). He was assuming an office that continued from generation to generation. And it was the handing on of the keys which symbolized the transfer of the prime minister's office to him as the successor. Thus, the notion of succession was built right into the image of the keys.

So when Jesus gave Peter the keys, he was entrusting his authority not only to Peter, but also to all of Peter's successors as well. It was as if Jesus was saying, "I give this authority not only to you, Peter, but also to all those who come after you in this office." Indeed, the symbolic keys were not meant for Peter alone, but were intended to be passed on to Peter's successors just as they were passed on from one prime minister to the next in the Davidic kingdom of old.

The idea of the papacy, therefore, has profound biblical roots. If we simply follow the biblical pattern about the prime minister in the Old Testament, the papacy makes a lot of sense. In the Davidic kingdom of old, the kings had a prime minister

The keys symbolized how the Davidic king vested the prime minister with his very authority.

in charge of the day-to-day affairs of the kingdom. And the keys of the kingdom symbolized that position. So if Jesus is the king and he's announcing the fulfillment of the Davidic kingdom, we'd expect him to have his prime minister! That's just what we would expect. And the fact that Jesus explicitly draws upon the imagery from Isaiah 22 about the keys of the kingdom makes this point even clearer: he's clearly establishing Peter as the prime minister, the one who will represent him in overseeing his kingdom.

This is why the Catholic Church has always taught that Peter's successor—the pope—serves as the "Vicar of Christ" and preeminent shepherd of God's people (cf. CCC 882). As the modern-day successor of Peter and bearer of "the keys," the pope stands as the current prime minister in Christ's kingdom. The pope is the King's representative here on earth. As the prime minister, he is vested with Jesus' authority and leads God's people in Christ's name. And like the prime minister Eliakim, who was a father figure in the kingdom of David (cf. Is. 22:21), the pope leads us as our "Holy Father" in the New Covenant kingdom of Jesus, the Church.

QUESTIONS FOR DISCUSSION

1. What is the importance of name changes in the Bible?

2. Read Matthew 16:13–18. Consider the significance of Simon's name being changed to Peter. Peter's name means "rock." What rock might Jesus be referring to when he calls Peter the rock upon which he will build the Church and the gates of death shall not prevail against it? What might this say about Peter's role in the Church?

3. Jesus also gave Peter "the keys of the kingdom of heaven" (Mt. 16:19). What did the "keys" of the Davidic kingdom symbolize in the Old Testament? (Read Isaiah 22:15–23). How might this background shed light on Peter's role in Christ's kingdom?

4. Respond to the following question: "Jesus might have given Peter a unique authoritative position in the kingdom, but the Scriptures nowhere teach that this position was meant to be passed on to successors. Where do the Scriptures say anything about an ongoing papacy with Peter having successors?"

5. How do people today view the idea of the papacy? Why might some people have difficulty accepting the pope as Christ's representative ruler and head of the Church?

6. How might the biblical foundations for the papacy discussed in this chapter make it easier for people to understand the essential role of the pope in Christ's kingdom?

Chapter 10

The Secret of the Messiah

$$\boxed{\text{M A T T H E W} \quad 1\,6\,:\,2\,0\,-\,2\,1\,:\,1\,1}$$

"Ssshhhh. . . . Don't tell anyone yet!"

That is basically what Jesus told the twelve apostles once they realized that he was the Messiah. In the last chapter, we saw that Simon Peter was the first person to declare explicitly that Jesus was the long-awaited Davidic king. Yet right after this exciting moment, Jesus did something which on the surface doesn't seem to make much sense: "Then he strictly charged the disciples to tell no one that he was the Christ" (Mt. 16:20).

Why would Jesus be so secretive? Didn't he want people to know his messianic identity? Jesus' push for secrecy is understandable when we consider the first-century Jewish context. Recall how "messiah" means "anointed one," referring to the anointing of a king. If word got out that he was explicitly claiming to be a king, Jesus would have attracted the wrong sort of attention. Given the political and militaristic emphasis attached to the Jewish messianic hopes in Jesus' day, such a public proclamation of his messiahship might have put him in a dangerous situation. Anyone gathering a large group of followers and then claiming to be their anointed king would have been considered a threat to the foreign powers that ruled the land. In fact, the last time would-be messiahs had entered the scene, just one generation before Jesus, their movements had been swiftly squashed by Herod and the Roman armies, and the leaders had been executed. Jesus was not ready for that quite yet. Although his time would come soon, he still had some work to do in his kingdom-building plan.

One such task involved redefining for his disciples the popular notion of messiahship, divesting it of the violent political and militaristic connotations it carried in many sectors of first-century Judaism. Many Jews in this time longed for a revolutionary messiah because they thought their problem centered primarily on the Roman occupation. Jesus, however, knew that Israel's problem was much deeper. He knew Israel was suffering from an oppressive force that was much more devastating than Roman soldiers or Caesar's taxes. The real problem facing Israel—and the rest of the world— was sin. Oppressive regimes, violent governments, and unjust economic structures were only symptoms of the much more serious illness of human sinfulness. The only way the external societal structures of Israel would be changed was through an internal transformation, beginning right in their own hearts. Political, social, and economic liberation would only be accomplished through the ultimate liberation from sin. And that is the type of freedom Jesus offered Israel as the Messiah-King.

He had much work to do, however, in explaining his mission as the Messiah, and he began with his own disciples. Even they were not immune to the popular way of envisioning the Messiah primarily through worldly political and militaristic lenses. One can imagine what they were thinking once they realized that their own leader was Israel's Messiah. What exhilaration and anticipation must have filled their hearts! Jesus was the one spoken of by the prophets—the one who would rise victoriously over Israel's enemies and restore the kingdom. Since Jesus had invited them to be co-leaders of his movement, the apostles probably hoped to be given high-ranking positions once the kingdom was established.

Much to their dismay, Jesus had another type of kingdom in mind, one that he wanted his apostles to understand. Notice how, immediately after Peter's recognition that Jesus was the Messiah, Our Lord painted a stark picture of what kind of Messiah he was to be. Just after Peter's great profession of faith, Jesus began telling the disciples about his upcoming death in Jerusalem:

> *From that time* Jesus began to show his disciples that he must go to Jerusalem and suffer many things from the elders and chief priests and scribes, and be killed, and on the third day be raised. (Mt. 16:21)

Think of what a shock this must have been to the apostles! What kind of Messiah was *this*? How could the Messiah be killed? Even Peter—who was just praised for recognizing Jesus as the promised Messiah—could not comprehend the idea of the Messiah dying at the hands of his enemies: "God forbid, Lord! This shall never happen to you" (Mt. 16:22).

This was the first time Jesus spoke to the apostles about his future death, and this difficult conversation could not have come at a more strategic time. Now that it was clear to his disciples that he was indeed the Messiah, Jesus needed to stress to them that his royal reign would be established not on the battlefield or in the political arena, but through his death on the Cross. So right away he warned the apostles to think twice before vying for offices in his kingdom. Far from being able to ride the Messiah's coattails into the kingdom, the apostles faced a radical challenge if they wished to participate in Jesus' reign:

> If any man would come after me, let him deny himself and take up his cross and follow me. For whoever would save his life will lose it, and whoever loses his life for my sake will find it. (Mt. 16:24–25)

This image of picking up a cross would have been completely shocking. The cross was a most horrific image of Roman execution. It brought to mind the most shameful, torturous way to be killed: crucifixion. We saw how Peter was already taken aback when Jesus told them he was going to be killed. Now Jesus tells the disciples what kind of death he's going to face—a death on a cross! And on top of that, he tells his disciples that they, too, needed to take up a cross if they want to follow him. Such a statement would be like saying in the modern world, "Pick up your guillotine and follow me." or "Pick up your electric chair and follow me." Will the disciples be able to follow him this far?

Such a statement would be like saying, "Pick up your electric chair and follow me."

THE TRANSFIGURATION

Six days after this earth-shattering revelation about the Cross, Jesus takes three of his disciples—Peter, James, and John—up a high mountain where they will see him transfigured. His face shines like the sun, his garments become white as light, a cloud overshadows them and the heavenly voice says, "This is my beloved Son, with whom I am well pleased; listen to him" (17:1–5).

What's the point of this spectacular display of Christ's glory? And why are these three apostles chosen to get front row seats for this event? Jesus is preparing them for the trials coming their way in Jerusalem. These men who have just learned that Jesus is the true messiah will see Jesus betrayed by Judas and arrested by soldiers in Gethsemane. There in Jerusalem, Jesus will be mocked, beaten, condemned, scourged and eventually crucified on Calvary. In fact, these same three apostles will be singled out on another mountain, the Mount of Olives, at the start of Christ's Passion. On the night before he dies, Jesus will go to the garden of Gethsemane on the Mount of Olives and will invite Peter, James, and John to be close to him while he prays in his agony, getting ready for all that is about to unfold in his Passion.

So why did Jesus give Peter, James, and John a glimpse of his divine glory in the Transfiguration? To prepare them for what they will witness when they are with him in Gethsemane—so that when they start to face all that Christ will endure in his Passion, they might be strengthened by the memory of the Transfiguration and remain confident that he really is the Son of God.

This point is expressed beautifully in a prayer from the Byzantine Liturgy: "You were transfigured on the mountain, and your disciples, as much as they were capable of it, beheld your glory, O Christ our God, so that when they should see you crucified they would understand that your passion was voluntary, and proclaim to the world that you truly are the splendor of the Father."[1]

JOURNEY TOWARD JERUSALEM

From this point on, Jesus' movement in Galilee picked up a new focus. In Israel's history, Jewish kings reigned from Jerusalem. Therefore, if Jesus was the Messiah-King, he must go to the capital city to be enthroned. This is why Jesus begins speaking of his death in Jeru-

---

[1] Byzantine Liturgy, Feast of the Transfiguration, *Kontakion*. As cited in CCC 555.

salem and taking his movement in the direction of the holy city.

Along the way, we see him continuing to redefine the notion of the Messiah and the kingdom for his apostles. He emphasizes how his reign will be quite different from the world's view of governing authority. In Matthew 18:1–4, Jesus extols certain qualities that few government leaders would see as essential to their authority. For Jesus, humility and childlikeness are fundamental characteristics of his kingdom: "Whoever humbles himself like this child, he is the greatest in the kingdom" (Mt. 18:4). Another feature of the kingdom of Jesus is forgiveness and mercy. Peter asks how many times he should forgive someone who harms him. "Seven times?" Peter asks. Jesus said to him, "I do not say to you seven times, but seventy times seven" (Mt. 18:22). This kingdom of forgiveness would have stood in contrast with many Jewish groups that wanted revenge on their pagan enemies.

Yet even after Jesus spoke about his upcoming death and the self-sacrifice, humility, and forgiveness that are hallmarks of his kingdom, the apostles still did not get it. An episode in Matthew 20 illustrates how the kingdom was still understood in the wrong categories. As Jesus and his followers were drawing nearer to Jerusalem, the mother of James and John approached Jesus on her knees with an amazing request: "Command that these two sons of mine may sit, one at your right hand and one at your left, in your kingdom" (Mt. 20:21). Not understanding the true nature of the kingdom and the price Jesus would pay for it, the mother of these two apostles asked Jesus to give her sons the first places in his kingdom.

Jesus uses this opportunity to emphasize once again what his kingdom is really all about. He turns to the apostles and asks, "Are you able to drink the cup that I am to drink?" referring to his imminent suffering and death (Mt. 20:22). Jesus then contrasts his kingdom with the kingdoms of the world:

> You know that the rulers of the Gentiles lord it over them, and their great men exercise authority over them. It shall not be so among you; but whoever would be great among you must be your servant, and whoever would be first among you must be your slave; even as the Son of man came not to be served but to serve, and to give his life as a ransom for many. (Mt. 20:25–28)

Humility, service, forgiveness, and sacrificial love. Jesus constantly returned to these themes in his teachings about the kingdom on the way to Jerusalem. Although many Jews wanted a military king who would topple the pagan nations oppressing them, Jesus knew that the solution to the sin of the Gentiles was not destroying their armies, but converting their hearts. Indeed, this was Israel's mission from the very beginning. God called their founding father Abraham and his descendants (the Israelites) to be the instrument for bringing blessing to a broken world. Israel was not called to fight off the world but to be light to the world. And Jesus knew it would only be through serving the

Gentiles, forgiving them, and loving them that even the most wicked of nations could be won over to worship the one true God.

THE COMING OF THE KING

Finally, Jesus arrives at Jerusalem (cf. Mt. 21:1–11). Here we come to a famous scene from the Gospels with which Catholics are quite familiar. The drama of "Palm Sunday" is relived every year in the liturgy when Catholics carry branches and process into church, recalling Jesus' procession into Jerusalem with the people greeting him as "the Son of David" and waving palm branches like they did when Judas Maccabeus freed the city from the Syrians (cf. 2 Mac. 10:7).

Notice how the people of Jerusalem gave Jesus a royal greeting. They, in a sense, rolled out a royal carpet for their monarch by spreading out branches and their garments on the ground where Jesus would walk—a custom

> *Jesus, without saying a word, was shouting out, "Zechariah 9:9 is coming to fulfillment in me!"*

ancient Jews did for kings in the Davidic monarchy (cf. 2 Kings 9:13). They called Jesus "the Son of David" and sang "Blessed is he who comes in the name of the Lord! Hosanna in the highest!" (Mt. 21:9).

But why did the people suddenly give Jesus all this royal treatment? If Jesus instructed his disciples to keep his messianic identity somewhat quiet, why do the people come out to honor him as their king?

It all has to do with the donkey.

The fact that Jesus chose to enter Jerusalem riding on a donkey is quite significant. This little detail alone tells us something important is about to happen. Nowhere else in the Gospel do we read about Jesus traveling on an animal. Everywhere else he traveled, Jesus went on foot over land or on boat over sea (and even then, he sometimes walked on the water!). But we never find him asking to ride on a donkey, or any other animal, except when he enters Jerusalem on this day. Why this new mode of transportation?

A key prophecy of Zechariah helps to illuminate this scene. Zechariah 9:9–10 foretells how the Messiah will enter Jerusalem riding on a donkey:

> Rejoice greatly, O daughter of Zion!
> Shout aloud, O daughter of Jerusalem!
> *Behold, your king comes to you;*
> triumphant and victorious is he,
>   *humble and riding on a donkey,*
> *on a colt the foal of a donkey....*
> [H]e shall command peace to the nations;
> his dominion shall be from sea to sea,
> and from the River to the ends of the earth.

Jesus deliberately chose to enter Jerusalem in this way in order to bring to mind Zechariah 9:9, a passage which the Jews knew very well. This prophecy summed up many of their hopes for the Messiah—the one who would rescue them from their oppressors. By riding into the holy city on a donkey, Jesus, without saying a single word, was shouting out, "I am the Messiah-King coming to be enthroned in Jerusalem! Zechariah 9:9 is coming to fulfillment in me!" If there were any question about Jesus' messianic claims, this action removed all doubt. Zechariah 9:9 was being fulfilled right there before their eyes. In this action, Jesus boldly and explicitly proclaimed that he was the Messiah. No wonder the crowds welcomed him into the holy city with such enthusiasm!

We saw earlier, however, that if Jesus were to publicly proclaim his messianic identity, he would quickly find himself in big trouble. With Pilate and the Romans ready to crush any rising revolutionaries or rival kings, a claim to messiahship would likely bring about an early end to his ministry and his very life. But after having laid the foundations for his kingdom, Jesus was now ready to make that bold move of announcing himself to be Israel's long-awaited Messiah-King. He had invested the apostles with his authority (Mt. 10), established Peter as the prime minister in the kingdom (Mt. 16), and trained his disciples on the true nature of the kingdom he was building (Mt. 16–20). Now at Jerusalem, Jesus rides in on a donkey symbolically declaring himself to be the Messiah . . . and in a few days he will pay the price.

Questions for Discussion

1. Read Matthew 16:20. Why do you think Jesus wanted to keep his messianic identity secret?

2. On the journey to Jerusalem, Jesus tries to reshape his apostles' view of what it means to be a leader in his kingdom. What do the following passages say about Jesus' vision for true discipleship? Matthew 16:24–28; 18:1–4; 18:21–22; 20:20–28

3. How does this vision of leadership differ from modern-day views? Which is more effective? Why?

4. Based on Jesus' teachings about leadership in his kingdom, how can you be a more effective leader for Christ in your family? At work? In your parish? In your community?

5. Jesus rides into Jerusalem on a donkey. What is Jesus symbolically saying about himself in this action (read Zechariah 9:9–11)? What will happen to him later that week as a result of this? Why?

Chapter 11

Jesus, the Temple, and the End Times

MATTHEW 21:12–25:46

IMAGINE GAZING UPON a building which makes up about one-fourth of an entire city and occupies an area equivalent to thirty-five football fields. That's what Jewish pilgrims would see when they approached the gigantic Temple to worship the one, true God. It has been said that the Temple in Jerusalem was not just a large building in one part of the city. It was more like "Jerusalem was a Temple with a city around it!"[1]

The immensity of the Temple is not surprising, considering the fact that this sacred building—and all

---

[1] N.T. Wright, *The Original Jesus* (Oxford: Lion Publishing, 1996), 57–58.

that it stood for—was the very center of Jewish life. This was the place where the God of the universe came to meet his chosen people. The Jews believed that the Temple actually housed God's awesome presence in its innermost chamber called the Holy of Holies. As the connecting point between heaven and earth, the Temple came to be known as "the navel of the world" and the center of the whole cosmos—the place where God's holiness radiated outward to the rest of creation.[2]

Indeed, the Jews believed their Temple to be a symbol for the entire world, a miniature replica of the universe made in architecture. What went on in the sacred space of the Temple—sacrifice, worship, and the dwelling of God's presence—was a reminder for God's people of the praise and worship that should resound from all corners of the world.

In addition to being the focal point for worship and sacrifice, the Temple also served as the center for Jewish government, their judicial system, and even much of their trade and economics. The Temple in Jerusalem was the first-century Jewish equivalent of the Vatican, White House, Supreme Court, and Wall Street all wrapped into one. In short, the Temple was everything to the Jews. It stood out as the number one symbol for their national identity.

So why did Jesus go in there and turn everything upside down?

[2] Marcus J. Borg, *Conflict, Holiness and Politics in the Teachings of Jesus* (Harrisburg, PA: Trinity Press International, 1998), 75–76.

KINGSHIP AND THE TEMPLE

Some of Israel's most famous kings were known for helping build, purify, or defend the Temple. David came up with the idea for the first Temple. His son Solomon built it and dedicated it to the Lord. Great reformer kings such as Hezekiah and Josiah built their renewals around restoring true worship in the Tem-

The Temple was the Jewish equivalent of the Vatican, White House, Supreme Court, and Wall Street all wrapped into one.

ple. Though not a Davidic heir, Judas Maccabeus won a century-long dynasty for his family because he cleansed the Temple from the pagan idolatry of the Syrians. And Herod, who was not a true Jew and received his throne from the Romans, tried to legitimize his claim to kingship in Judea by rebuilding the Temple in great splendor. As we can see, kingship and the Temple went hand in hand in Israel's history.

One of the first things Jesus did when he arrived in Jerusalem was to enter the Temple. There he performed the powerful, dramatic action of turning over the tables of the moneychangers—an action which must be understood in light of Israel's prophetic tradition. Israel's prophets often communicated not just in words, but in powerful symbolic actions. For example, six centuries before Christ, when the Temple elders were corrupt and the Jerusalem leaders were leading the people away from God's covenant, the prophet Jeremiah took a clay jar to the elders of Jerusalem and Temple priests and smashed it in front of them. He explained that what he just did with the jar symbolized what God would do with Jerusalem and the Temple because of their unfaithfulness (cf. Jer. 19:10–11). His symbolic action foretold the destruction of the Temple by Babylon in 586 BC.

We will now see how Jesus performed a similar act of judgment on the Temple when he overturned the tables of the moneychangers, thereby inhibiting people from buying and selling in the Temple courts.

When Jews traveled to Jerusalem to worship in the Temple, they needed to present the priests with unblemished animals to be offered in sacrifice. Rather than bring cattle, sheep, or goats with them on a long journey, they generally bought their animals in Jerusalem. But to make this purchase, they needed to obtain the local currency for doing business at the Temple. This is why there were moneychangers' tables in the Temple courts. Indeed, stopping at the moneychangers' tables was often the first important step pilgrims would take in the long process of worshiping in the temple. They would (a) *exchange their money* to the right local coinage so that (b) they could *buy their animals* and then (c) *present the animals to the priests*, who (d) would *offer the animals in sacrifice* on their behalf in the temple.

By turning all the moneychangers' tables upside down, Jesus prevented anyone from getting the proper coinage. With no currency exchange, animals could not be bought and, consequently, sacrifices could not be offered. In one broad stroke, Jesus put a dramatic halt to the entire Temple system for a few hours that day— prefiguring how all sacrifices would soon cease when the Temple would be destroyed forever. Like Jeremiah who smashed the clay jar, Jesus' actions symbolized how the Jerusalem Temple would soon be destroyed by the Romans, which is exactly what happened in AD 70.

But why would Jesus condemn the Temple in this way? He explained his actions, saying: "It is written, 'My house shall be called a house of prayer'; but you make it a den of robbers" (Mt. 21:13). In these cryptic words, Jesus is referring to two important Old Testament passages.

First, Jesus is quoting a passage from Isaiah 56, which should be read in its context. Isaiah 56 emphasized the universality of God's plan of salvation. It described how the Lord will gather all kinds of people, even the Gentiles, to himself in the New Covenant era. In fact, the verse which Jesus quoted tells how God wants peoples from all nations to come to the Jerusalem Temple to worship him: "[M]y house shall be called a house of prayer *for all peoples*" (Is. 56:7). Jesus quotes Isaiah 56 in order to recall Israel's mission to gather *all peoples* together to worship the one true God.

However, rather than being a source of bringing in the Gentiles, the Temple in Jesus' day had become a wall of division keeping them out. No other institution stood out more as Israel's national identity marker, setting the Jews apart from the non-Jews. An inscription over the entryway to the Temple's inner courts made the point crystal clear: "No alien may enter within the barrier and wall around the Temple. Whoever is caught is alone responsible for the death which follows."[3]

---

[3] Borg, *Conflict, Holiness and Politics*, 76.

How's *that* for a sign of hospitality! Jesus criticizes the way the temple had become a source of division and in his words reminds the temple leaders that God's house was meant to be "a house of prayer for all the nations," not just the Jews (Is. 56:7).

Second, when Jesus describes the temple becoming a "den of robbers," he is recalling Jeremiah's critique of the people of Jerusalem in his own day—men who were living double lives. They would steal, murder, commit adultery, and worship idols, but still come to the Lord in the Temple, thinking God would deliver them even if they didn't repent of their wicked ways. But Jeremiah foretold how God would bring judgment on them and how the temple would be destroyed because they had turned God's house into a "den of robbers" (Jer. 7:8–15).

So when Jesus uses the words "den of robbers," he's recalling how Jeremiah called the people of Jerusalem to repent and warned about the temple's destruction if they didn't. Jesus is, therefore, coming to Jerusalem as a new Jeremiah. Just as Jeremiah foretold the destruction of the temple in the sixth century BC and condemned the city for turning God's house into a den of robbers, so Jesus is predicting the destruction of the temple in his own day and condemning the Jerusalem leaders for turning the house of the Lord into a "den of robbers" once more.

But in what sense had the temple become a "den of robbers" in Jesus' day? Many interpret Jesus' statement to be a denunciation of the commercialism which supposedly had entered God's holy house. However, the Greek word for "robbers" (*lestes*) in the New Testament text actually referred to much more than swindling merchants who exploited people while doing business. Rather, it referred to those who killed and destroyed while stealing. In the first century, the word *lestes* could be used to describe revolutionaries who wanted to take up arms against the Romans. Indeed, the Temple eventually became the focal point for Israel's resistance to Rome in the years leading up to its destruction in AD 70.

So when Jesus said, "You made this house a den of *lestes*," he was not primarily condemning economic exploitation. He was saying that the Jerusalem Temple was meant to be a light to the nations, a house of prayer for all peoples, but its leaders would soon make it a point of focus for revolutionaries.

SECOND COMING

Jesus' frustrations with the Temple are evident when he exited the building with his apostles another time later that week. The apostles were admiring the magnificent structures of the Temple, which was famously known as one of the most impressive buildings of the ancient world. Just at that moment, however, Jesus tells them of something shocking that was soon to happen there. This massive building soon would be destroyed: "Truly, I say to you, there will not be left here one stone upon another, that will not be thrown down" (Mt. 24:2).

The apostles ask him when this would take place and what would be the signs. Jesus responds with a lengthy apocalyptic discourse. He gives ominous warnings about wars, earthquakes, famines, and persecutions coming. He speaks about the sun and moon darkening, stars falling from the sky, and the need to flee from the city to the mountains. He even gives a timetable for when all this would occur: "Truly, I say to you, this generation will not pass away till all these things take place" (Mt. 24:34).

Many interpret Jesus' words in this passage as referring primarily to his second coming at the end of the world. However, there is one problem with this interpretation: Jesus said these events would take place within one generation. Yet, many generations have passed since Jesus spoke these words and we know the stars, in fact, did not fall, and the sun and moon continue to appear each day to be illuminating the sky. So did Jesus get the timing for the end of the world wrong?

No. We have to understand Jesus' words not by our own twenty-first-century worldview, but in the way they would have been understood in his first century Jewish culture. For many of us Christians today, if we hear someone talk about the sun and moon no longer giving light, stars falling from the sky and the Son of man coming on the clouds of heaven, we are likely to think the person is talking about the end of the world. *But that's not how ancient Jews would have understood this imagery.* They would have realized Jesus was using traditional Jewish apocalyptic imagery—imagery that had been used many times before in their Scriptures. And it was used in the Old Testament not in a literalistic way to portray the dramatic events surrounding the destruction of the world, but as metaphors describing the fall of great empires, powers, and institutions that were corrupt and hostile to God's people.

136

Today, people in the USA might talk about the start of their country's revolutionary war as "the shot heard around the world." No one thinks that the opening gunshot which sparked the American revolutionary war was actually heard in Paris, Cairo, and Tokyo. It's just a metaphor. It's a metaphor describing how the start of this war had such a political, social and economic impact not just for the nation of the United States of America, but for many countries around the world. It's as if the shot was heard around the world. Similarly, Israel's prophets knew good metaphors and often used them. They often used cataclysmic language and cosmic metaphors like this to depict how God would rid the world of powerful wicked rulers, bringing their reigns to an end.

For example, when speaking about the judgment that would fall upon a wicked Jerusalem, the prophet Ezekiel used the imagery of famine, pestilence, and wars, and he warned the Jews to escape to the mountains. He used such language to describe the horror Jerusalem would face when the Babylonians would soon come in and crush the city (cf. Ezek. 7:14–16). Similarly, the prophets Jeremiah and Zechariah called for Jews to flee from Babylon on the day when Yahweh would liberate and vindicate his people by demolishing the Babylonian empire (cf. Jer. 50:8, 28; Zech. 2:6–8). Other prophets used the image of earthquakes to depict great nations which soon would tumble to the ground. They also employed the cataclysmic imagery of the sun and moon darkening and stars falling from the sky to describe how Israel's enemies, such as Babylon and Egypt, would lose their strength and fall from power (cf. Is. 13:1, 10; 14:12;

Ezek. 32:7–8; Joel 2:10). The sudden fall of a dominant empire or a powerful king was so surprising, so shocking, that the prophets likened it to a star falling from the sky or the sun no longer giving its light.

Israel's prophets routinely spoke this way to portray God's intervention in the history of the world's great powers as dramatic, "earth-shaking" events. Although this prophetic imagery was not meant to describe the end of *the* world, it certainly emphasized the imminent end of *a* world—the end of the Babylonian world, the Egyptian world, or the world of other powers who opposed God's people.

Standing in that same prophetic tradition, Jesus spoke of famines, wars, earthquakes, people fleeing, the sun and moon darkening, and stars falling from the sky. And he did so in the context of his predicting the destruction of the Temple (cf. Mt. 24:2). Like the prophets before him, Jesus employed these catastrophic images to prophetically foretell how God was coming in judgment on Israel's enemies. However, Jesus did so with an ironic twist. This time, the enemies of God's people were not Babylon, Assyria, Egypt, or even Rome. The enemies of God's people were their own leaders of the Jerusalem Temple! God's judgment now would fall upon the Temple leaders who had become corrupt and were leading the people away from the true Messiah-King, Jesus.

Jesus prophesied that the Temple would be de-

> *The sudden fall of a powerful king was so shocking that the prophets likened it to a star falling from the sky.*

stroyed within one generation, and his prediction was right on the money. For the Jews, a generation was forty years. About forty years after Jesus spoke these words, Roman troops raided Jerusalem, burned down the city, and destroyed the Temple in AD 70—all taking place within a generation, just as he had foretold.

Think about what the end of the Temple would mean. We earlier saw how the Temple summed up Israel's entire life and covenant with God. Practically all aspects of Israel's relationship with Yahweh in the Old Covenant were related to the Temple. Insofar as the Temple summed up the Old Covenant, the end of the Temple would symbolize the end of the Old Covenant world. Indeed, that is exactly what we have seen Jesus bringing about: the end of the old, so he could usher in the new.

Still, there may be a secondary sense in which Jesus' words can be seen as pointing also to the end of the physical world. Recall how the Jews viewed their Temple as the center of the universe and as a symbol for the entire cosmos. As such, the destruction of the Temple might signify what the end of the world may be like. While Jesus' words point primarily to the demise of the Temple in AD 70, they also prefigure what could happen to the entire cosmos at the end of time.[4]

---

[4] George Montague notes how the destruction of the Temple and the end of the world could have been closely associated in Jesus' mind, "for Jews considered the Temple to be one of the foundations of the world, and the end of the one would be the end of the other." George T. Montague, S.M., *Companion God* (New York: Paulist Press, 1989), 262.

QUESTIONS FOR DISCUSSION

1. In Matthew 21:12–13, Jesus enters the Temple and overturns the tables of the moneychangers. What was the purpose of the moneychangers in the Temple? Why were they so important for the Temple's sacrificial system?

2. What was Jesus symbolically saying about the Temple when he overturned the moneychangers' tables? Consider what Jesus says in Matthew 21:13. If the Temple was God's house and the very center of Israel's life, why was Jesus condemning it?

3. In his discourse in Matthew 24:4–35, Jesus uses an array of cataclysmic images such as earthquakes, fleeing to the mountains, and the sun, moon, and stars darkening to describe some type of earth-shattering event. To understand the event to which Jesus was referring, consider the following questions:

- Matthew 24:1–2 sets the context for his apocalyptic discourse in the rest of the chapter. What is Jesus speaking about in Matthew 24:1–2?
- How do the Old Testament prophets use similar cosmic imagery in the following passages: Isaiah 13:1, 9–10; 14:4, 12; Ezekiel 32:1–2, 7–8? Is this Old Testament prophetic imagery of the sun, moon, and stars darkening and falling from the sky primarily used to describe the end of the physical world, or God's coming in judgment upon a particular ruler or nation?

- In light of this background, how should we interpret Jesus' use of similar language in Matthew 24:29? Who might God be coming to judge?
- According to verse 34, when does Jesus say all these events will take place?
- Certainly, the world was not destroyed in that time period. So what was Jesus referring to? What was actually destroyed within that time period?

Chapter 12

The Trial of the King

MATTHEW 26:1–27:26

JESUS' ACTIONS were bound to get him in trouble sooner or later. In those days, someone couldn't just ride into Jerusalem, signal messianic fulfillment, and then expect to go unnoticed. Nor could one march into the holy Temple to turn everything upside down, condemn it, and predict its destruction without attracting the wrong sort of attention.

The crowds may have rejoiced at his coming to Jerusalem and welcomed him as a king (cf. Mt. 21:1–11), but the Jewish authorities were anxious. How could they get excited about a growing movement which challenged their authority and shook the nation's very identity? In their eyes, Jesus' entire movement stood in

143

opposition to the Temple and the Torah. They saw him leading the people away from God's holy house and from God's sacred law. They would ask: "How could this man be the Messiah? He eats with sinners, disregards the purity laws, and forgives sins on his own authority. And who does he think he is, condemning God's holy Temple in this way?" They probably saw Jesus as a false prophet, leading the people astray. Therefore, he had to be stopped (cf. Deut. 13:1–5).

During that tumultuous week in Jerusalem, Jesus seemed to be aware that his days were numbered. He even told parables which prefigured his upcoming death. For example, Jesus told a story to the chief priests about a landowner who let his vineyard be run by tenants. When the landowner sent his servants to collect the fruit from the land, the tenants killed each of the servants one by one. Finally, the landowner decided to send his own son, saying, "They will respect my son." But the tenants murdered even the son. In the end, the tenants were driven off the land and killed for their wickedness (cf. Mt. 21:33–46).

This story would have sounded quite familiar to the chief priests who were listening. Jesus was building on a traditional Jewish story (taken from Isaiah 5) in which the vineyard symbolized Israel, the landowner represented God, and God was looking for Israel to bear good fruit.

But Jesus adds his own twist to the story, introducing a few new characters. The landowner entrusts the *tenants* with the vineyard, but they have not yielded good fruit for the landowner. These tenants represent the leaders of

Israel, who are supposed to be caring for the nation but have not led them to bear fruit.

Jesus also adds the *servants* who were sent by the landowner to collect the fruit. These represent the many prophets whom God sent throughout the years to challenge Israel to be faithful and fruitful, living out its calling to be light to the nations. But Israel did not listen to them. They rejected the prophets and did not repent.

The third new character is *the landowner's son*, who, of course, represents Jesus himself. The point here is that God is now sending one last messenger—one who surpasses all the other prophets who had come before. This time, God is sending his own Son, Jesus. Sadly, the leaders of Israel will kill him, too.

Upon hearing the story, the chief priests suddenly realize that Jesus is speaking about them (cf. Mt. 21:45). They were like the tenants who had rejected God's prophets, and now they were about to kill the landowner's son. As a result, they would be punished like the tenants in the story. Jesus said to them, "Therefore I tell you, the kingdom of God will be taken away from you and given to a nation producing the fruits of it" (Mt. 21:43).

ON TRIAL

With the help of the Apostle Judas, the chief priests and elders eventually arrest Jesus at night and bring him to trial before the high priest, Caiaphas, and the other Jewish leaders in Jerusalem (cf. Mt. 26:57–68).

First, the council tries to gather false testimony against him. Then, Jesus is accused of condemning the Temple. All the while, Jesus remained silent, offering no defense. Only once did he speak, and that was when the high priest stood up and commanded Jesus by oath to tell him one thing: "Tell us if you are the Messiah!" At that, Jesus finally responded and, in two short sentences, he turned their whole world completely upside down. He said, "You have said so. But I tell you, hereafter you will see the Son of man seated at the right hand of Power, and coming on the clouds of heaven" (Mt. 26:64).

At this, the high priest tears his robes in disgust and accuses Jesus of blasphemy, and the council members slap him, spit on him, strike him, and condemn him to death. A harsh punishment for two little sentences! What did Jesus say that got him into so much trouble? Why do the chief priests become so infuriated at these words? What made the council condemn him to death?

In speaking of the Son of man coming on the clouds of heaven, Jesus was alluding to a famous prophecy in the Book of Daniel. The prophet Daniel had a dream—perhaps it could be considered a nightmare—about four dreadful beasts who were devouring God's people: a lion with wings, a man-eating bear, a four-headed leopard, and a most fierce beast with ten horns and iron teeth. Each beast represented four powerful Gentile kingdoms which waged war on the Jewish people. Suddenly, a mysterious human figure appeared in the dream—"one like a Son of man" (Dan. 7:13). The beasts were then destroyed, while the Son of man was taken up to the throne of God and given authority to rule over all the nations.

This was a prophecy of great hope. In the vision, the Son of man represents God's faithful people who had suffered under one severe Gentile regime after another. But in the end, the Son of man eventually would be rescued by God and would triumph over the enemies. God's people finally would be freed, and they would share in his reign over all the nations.

In his trial before the high priest, Jesus evoked this vision of Daniel and associated himself with the Son of man. In this daring move, Jesus was claiming to be representing God's people, as the Son of man had done in Daniel's dream. This is particularly striking given the fact that he said this in front of the high priest and the Jerusalem council—the Jewish leaders who saw *themselves* as holding that representative role for the people. Right in their face and right in their headquarters in Jerusalem, Jesus daringly tells them that *he* is now playing that part. *He* is the Son of man, the true representative of God's people. And God would rescue *him* from his enemies and give *him* dominion over all the nations. Tough words from a poor defendant on trial, especially from one whose own life was on the line!

But that is not all. If Jesus was claiming to be the persecuted Son of man here in this trial before the chief priests, what was he saying about his accusers? In Jesus' astonishing retelling of this traditional story from Daniel, the leaders of Jerusalem have assumed the role of the beasts who persecute the Son of man. Now *they* are the enemies of the Jews because *they* are opposing the one whom God had sent to free God's people.

Can you feel the punch line? Jesus is saying that the leaders of Jerusalem have become like the Gentile monsters which have oppressed the Jews for centuries. The leaders of God's people have become the enemies of God's people. The chief priests have become the chief beasts.[1] Jesus simply could not have struck a lower blow to his accusers.[2]

Still, there's even more to Jesus' words. Jesus describing himself as "seated at the right hand of Power" and "coming on the clouds of heaven" is what provokes the chief priests the most. For these images are associated with God himself. Jesus claims he will sit on a throne in heaven like God and that he will come on the clouds like God. Indeed, in the Bible, clouds are often associated with God's holy presence. God draws near to his people and makes his presence known visibly in a pillar of cloud guiding the Israelites in the desert, in a cloud descending on Mount Sinai, a cloud overshadowing the holy sanctuary known as the Tabernacle, and a cloud filling the Temple in Jerusalem. For Jesus to say he is the Son of man "seated at the right hand of Power, and coming on the clouds of heaven" is to be implicitly pointing to his divinity. He associates himself with the same Almighty God who sits on a throne in heaven and who draws near to his people on earth *by coming on the clouds*. Jesus' claim to divinity here is what incites Caiaphas to tear his robe

---

[1] Chris Wright, *Knowing Jesus Through the Old Testament* (Downers Grove, IL: InterVarsity Press, 1992), 152–53.

[2] See Edward Sri, *No Greater Love: A Biblical Walk through Christ's Passion* (West Chester, PA: Ascension, 2019), 70–75.

and shout "Blasphemy!"—a direct insult against God that is punishable by death.[3]

HANDED OVER TO PILATE

Under Roman rule, the Jews did not have the authority to carry out an execution on their own. That's why the chief priests handed Jesus over to Pilate, the Roman governor who was in charge of the land.

Notice how Jesus' trial before Pilate is very different from his interrogation with Caiaphas. As the local leader for the Roman empire, Pilate was not concerned about what Jesus taught about the Temple. He was not interested in whether Jesus claimed to be the Son of man in Daniel 7 or what Jesus thought about the chief priests. Pilate basically had only one question for Jesus, and it was a political one: "Are you the King of the Jews?" (Mt. 27:11).

> *The chief priests have become the chief beasts.*

In the Roman world, there is no king but Caesar. Any opposition to Rome must be squashed immediately. Any rival king to the Emperor must be exterminated. So Pilate sought to determine if Jesus really was some type of rebel king, a real threat to the empire.

He quickly realized that Jesus was not the ordinary sort of revolutionary leader who threatened Roman rule. Pilate was used to dealing with revolutionaries and

---

[3] "If Jesus is claiming to be a *divine* Messiah who will be seated on a heavenly throne (like God) and come in on the clouds of heaven (also like God), then the charge of blasphemy makes sense." Brant Pitre, *The Case for Jesus* (New York: Image, 2016), 161.

could quickly tell Jesus was not one of them. He could see that the real reason the chief priests brought Jesus to him was due to a religious rivalry they had with Jesus (cf. Mt. 27:18).

Knowing Jesus' innocence, Pilate wanted to release him. But he could not withstand the pressure from the crowds who had been stirred up by the chief priests and were demanding that Jesus be crucified. John's Gospel tells us that the crowds even threatened Pilate, telling him that if he released a rebel-king, he would prove himself to be a traitorous governor, disloyal to Caesar: "If you release this man, you are not Caesar's friend; every one who makes himself a king sets himself against Caesar" (Jn. 19:12). The last thing Pilate would want would be for that type of accusation to reach Caesar's ears back home in Rome. Afraid of a riot and fearing for his own job, Pilate caved in and handed Jesus over to be crucified (cf. Mt. 27:26).

THE FINAL CHOICE

In the midst of the mounting pressure, Pilate offered to release one prisoner to the Jews, either Jesus or a man named Barabbas. "Whom do you want me to release for you, Barabbas or Jesus who is called Christ?" (Mt. 27:17). He left it to the crowd to decide, and they chose Barabbas, telling Pilate to send Jesus to the Cross.

Who was this mysterious prisoner named Barabbas? And why would the crowds choose him over Jesus? Barabbas means "son of the father." Besides giving us his name, however, Matthew doesn't say much about him. But he does give us one little description that is quite revealing. He tells us that Barabbas was "a notorious prisoner"—so notorious that Matthew, perhaps, could assume that his readers would have had no doubt which Barabbas he was talking about. It was the famous Barabbas who was imprisoned for murder during a revolt (cf. Mk. 15:7; Lk. 23:19; Jn. 18:40). Barabbas was a revolutionary.

So when Pilate stood before the crowds with this offer, the Jews were faced with one final choice: the rebel Barabbas or Jesus. But this wasn't just a choice between two different prisoners. It was a symbolic choice between two different ways of being Israel. Who was the true Israelite? Who was the true son of the Father?

Which road would the people follow? The way of Barabbas or the way of Jesus? The path of bitter nationalism or the path of welcoming in all the outcasts and Gentiles? The way of war, vengeance, and military action, or the way of peace, forgiveness, and the patient enduring of suffering?

Pilate basically had only one question for Jesus: "Are you the King of the Jews?"

Ultimately it came down to choosing between the way of the revolutionaries or the way of the Cross. The crowds chose the former, while Jesus was sent down the latter.

QUESTIONS FOR DISCUSSION

1. In Matthew 26:57–68, Jesus goes on trial before the Jewish council of leaders in Jerusalem known as the Sanhedrin. What were the charges brought against Jesus in his trial before the high priest? Why does the high priest Caiaphas accuse Jesus of blasphemy (Mt. 26:65)?

2. Read Matthew 27:15–26, Mark 15:7, Luke 23:18–19, and John 18:38–40. What was Barabbas known for? What movement in first-century Judaism would he have represented? What is the symbolism of the crowd's choosing Barabbas instead of Jesus?

3. Read Matthew 27:24–26. Why does Pilate give in to the crowd? Read John 19:12–16. What do you think Pilate is ultimately afraid of? What might have happened to Pilate if he released Jesus?

4. Like Pilate, we can be tempted to let our fears keep us from doing what we know is the right thing to do. What fears do you think sometimes keep people from standing up for what is true and doing the right thing? Why is this so? How can we avoid being a coward like Pilate? In what ways can we stand up for the truth more and do the right thing—even if we know it may cause us suffering?

Chapter 13

The Climax of the Cross

ROMAN CRUCIFIXION was a horrendous way to die. It didn't just bring a criminal to his death. It did so with the greatest possible pain and public humiliation.

The act itself was not intended to strike at vital organs or cause terminal bleeding. Rather, it was meant to cause a slow and painful death through shock or asphyxiation as the body's breathing muscles gradually collapsed—a process which sometimes took several days.

To inflict maximum humiliation, the condemned person was often stripped naked, scourged, and tied or nailed to a post. Then he was raised up high and ridiculed by those passing by. In the process, the people could see very clearly what happens to those who resist Roman rule.

All this sent a strong message to people like the Jews who were subject to the domination of the Roman Empire. It said, "We control your entire nation. We can do whatever we want with you. We can even take your body, nail it to a slab of wood, and make you suffer this excruciatingly painful death. Don't even think about rising up against us."

It is understandable why many Jews in the first century would have been puzzled by a crucified Messiah. They were expecting the Messiah to lead them in triumph over the foreign oppressors and bring freedom to the land. Many would have looked at Jesus dying on the Cross and said, "How could *this* be the Messiah? The Messiah was supposed to *defeat* the Romans, not be defeated *by* them!"

Far from appearing as a victorious king, Jesus would have seemed in many eyes to be more like a lost cause—a failure, another would-be messiah who let the people down. No wonder some people mocked him on Calvary, crying out: "If he is the king of Israel, let him come down from the Cross!" (cf. Mt. 27:39–44).

But if we take a closer look at the Cross, we'll discover that Christ's moment of defeat is actually his greatest victory, his utter debasement stands as his greatest exaltation, and his death on the Cross actually is his enthronement as Messiah-King.

Jesus gives us one important window to this mystery of the Cross at the Last Supper—where Jesus offers his body and blood as the new Passover lamb.

A New Passover

The fact that Jesus was handed over and crucified during the time of Passover would have been of great significance to the Jews of his day. This annual celebration was the feast of all Jewish feasts. It summed up Israel's history and fueled their hopes for a new era that would bring freedom from foreign oppression and forgiveness of Israel's sins.

One reason the Passover was so important is that it recalled the fateful night when God freed Israel from slavery in Egypt during the time of Moses. Despite several plagues which fell on the Egyptians, Pharaoh repeatedly refused to let the Israelites go. But on the night of that first Passover, God instructed the Israelites to sacrifice an unblemished lamb, eat its flesh, and mark their doorposts with the lamb's blood. Then all the first-born sons in Egypt were struck down that night, while the Israelite first-born sons were spared because Yahweh "passed over" the homes that had the mark of the lamb's blood (Ex. 12). After this tenth and most severe plague, Pharaoh finally released the Israelites from slavery, and the people fled Egypt in the night. That first Passover brought about Israel's redemption from slavery and helped forge their national identity as God's chosen people.

Subsequent generations of Israelites remembered

Could this be the Passover night when the Messiah would come?

this foundational event by celebrating the Passover feast. Once a year, they re-enacted that first Passover. They sacrificed a lamb and ate it in this sacred meal in order to express their solidarity with their deceased ancestors from the Exodus.

Another reason the Passover was so important was that it not only looked to the past, but also turned to the future as Jews would plea for Yahweh to vindicate his people once again. Especially in the time of Jesus, the Passover was associated with great messianic expectation and hope for a *new* exodus. What God did for Israel through Moses, he would do again through the Messiah. Just as God liberated the people from Pharaoh and the Egyptians, so he would free them from Herod, Pilate, and the Romans. And many Jews believed God would bring about this new exodus once again on a particular day of the year—on the day of Passover.

In fact, an ancient Passover poem used in synagogue liturgy depicts four great events in salvation history occurring on the same calendar day as the Passover feast: creation of the universe, the covenant with Abraham, and Israel's deliverance from Egypt all occurred on the night of the Passover. And according to this poem, it was on this same night that the future messianic king was expected to bring redemption to the Jews.[1]

Imagine the messianic expectation that must have

---

[1] This poem, called the "Poem of the Four Nights," is found in the targum *Neophyti*, an Aramaic paraphrase of the Old Testament used for synagogue worship. See *Neophyti* I, vol. 2 (Madrid-Barcelona, 1970), 312–13, as cited in Lucien Deiss, *It's the Lord's Supper* (London: Collins, 1975), 35.

filled the hearts of the disciples when Jesus instructed them to prepare the Passover meal. This must have
been the capstone in a week of mounting excitement.
The disciples already had watched their Master enter
the royal city of Jerusalem in royal fashion riding on
a donkey. They witnessed the crowds claim him as a
king. They saw him cleanse the Temple as some of Israel's great kings had done. And now, with Passover just
around the corner—and all the messianic hopes bound
up with this feast—some of the disciples preparing the
Passover meal were probably wondering if this was the
night when Jesus would carry out his ultimate messianic work: "Could this be *the* Passover of Passovers that
we've all been waiting for? Could this be the Passover
night when the Messiah would enact the new exodus
and rescue our people?"

What is most striking about the account of the Last
Supper is that the Passover lamb is nowhere mentioned
in the entire narrative. The eating of the lamb came at
the climax of the Passover feast. But just at the moment
when one would expect the lamb to be eaten, Jesus did
something rather surprising:

> Jesus took bread, and blessed, and broke it, and
> gave it to the disciples and said "Take, eat; this
> is my body." And he took a cup, and when he
> had given thanks he gave it to them, saying,
> "Drink of it, all of you; for this is my blood of
> the covenant, which is poured out for many for
> the forgiveness of sins." (Mt. 26:26–28)

Instead of focusing on the Passover lamb, Jesus spoke of *his* own body being eaten. Instead of pointing to the lamb's sacrificial blood, Jesus spoke of *his* own blood being poured out in sacrifice. What is the meaning of these mysterious words? Jesus dramatically pre-enacts what would take place on Good Friday. The breaking of bread expresses how Jesus' own body soon would be broken on the Cross. The cup of blood being poured out expresses how his own blood soon would be poured out on Calvary. Jesus is saying that he was like the Passover lamb. Just as the Passover lamb was offered up in sacrifice in order to free the Israelite first-born sons in Egypt, so Jesus will be offered in order to free God's first-born son, the people of Israel (cf. Ex. 4:22).

Another window into the mystery of the Cross is found in Jesus' mission as Israel's representative Messiah-King. Recall how in chapter four we saw that the Jews viewed their king as standing in the place of the entire nation. He was Israel's royal representative, summing up the entire people in himself, so much so that what happened to the king was understood as having happened to the people as a whole. Now we will see how Jesus, assuming that role as messianic representative, will bring Israel's history to its climax on the Cross and carry the people to their ultimate destiny.

To do this, we must first look at one element from Israel's tradition which probably shaped the way the Jews looked at their own tragic history and their hope for Israel's restoration more than anything else: the solemn covenant Israel made with God in the Old Testament Book of Deuteronomy.

We've already seen in chapter five how this foundational covenant, made just before the people entered the Promised Land, put before the Israelites two paths which would set the course of their history all the way up to the time of Jesus. One path was the way of faithfulness and covenant blessing, while the other was the way of unfaithfulness and destruction. Moses told the people that if they remained faithful to Yahweh, they would be blessed in the Promised Land. But if they proved unfaithful to the Lord, they would close themselves off from God's blessings and a series of curses would fall upon them. Fevers, illnesses, blindness, and leprosy would ravage the people. Famine, drought, and pestilence would cover the land. Foreign armies would constantly attack their nation.

The ultimate curse, however, was exile: Pagan empires would drive the Israelites out from the Promised Land and carry them away as slaves. Even their king would be handed over to the Gentiles, and Israel would be completely destroyed. With all this turmoil thrown onto Israel, it is no wonder that Moses described the horrible curses as a kind of covenant death: "I call heaven and earth to witness against you this day, that I have set before you life and death, blessing and curse; therefore choose life, that you and your descendants may live." (Deut. 30:19).

Unfortunately, Israel did not choose the way of covenant faithfulness. In rejecting the God who wanted to bless them, Israel knew that it had suffered the painful effects of life outside the blessing, just as Deuteronomy had foretold. As the prophet Daniel explained, this was the background for understanding Israel's sad state of affairs under foreign oppression: "[T]he curse and oath which are written in the law of Moses the servant of God have been poured out upon us, because we have sinned" (Dan. 9:11).

SALVATION FOR SINNERS

How did Christ's death on the Cross free God's people from this mess? Sometimes Jesus' work on Calvary is presented as if he simply stepped in and took our punishment by being crucified. In this perspective, Jesus was an innocent victim who took our penalty for us, freeing us from the divine wrath which we, as sinners, truly deserved.

The Scriptures, however, tell us there is something more to the mystery of the Cross. As the people's messianic representative, Jesus did not die simply as a *substitute* for Israel, but *in solidarity with* Israel, especially in its lowest points. Throughout his ministry, Jesus went out to the darkest corners of the nation to meet the people in the places where the suffering was most acute and the powers of evil ran most rampant. He reached out to the blind and the lame. He touched the untouchable lepers and dead bodies. He entered into table fellowship with some of the most renowned sinners. He even approached demoniacs to free them from the power of Satan.

Every step of the way, Jesus identified himself with the sinners and outcasts who were considered ritually impure and estranged from the covenant. Yet, instead of being defiled by them, Jesus' holiness overpowered their impurities, bringing physical healing and covenant restoration. In this way, Jesus met the people of Israel in the valley of their suffering and sin in order to unite himself to them in their dismal condition and lift them up to blessing and new life.

All this came to a climax on the Cross. There, Jesus plunged into the depths of Israel's agony. As Israel's representative Messiah-King, he entered into the people's intense suffering under foreign oppression as he himself was taken away and crucified by the Gentile enemies. And there on the Cross, Jesus took the ultimate step of meeting Israel at its lowest point of all—its curse of death. Uniting himself to Israel in its estrangement from God and in its covenantal death, Jesus could lift the people out of the grave in the Resurrection. Joining himself to the depths of Israel's sufferings on Good Friday, he could raise them up with him on Easter Sunday. This was the real victory of the Messiah. He set the people free, just as the prophets had foretold, but not in the way many expected. It was not a triumph over Caesar, Herod, and the Roman empire, but a victory over the real enemies of the Jews: sin, death, and the forces of evil. It was a battle won not by swords and soldiers, but by the patient enduring of suffering and the radical outpouring of love and forgiveness. It was the end of the most profound exile Israel ever experienced—the deeper, spiritual exile of being separated from God.

Israel, however, was not the only nation that Jesus came to rescue. *All* the children of Adam suffered from a life estranged from God and cut off from his blessing. All humanity stood in need of Christ's Redemption. This is seen in how Jesus enters the story of the human family's first father, Adam. Consider the many ways the curses of Adam prefigure what Christ endured on Good Friday.

Adam was tested by the devil in the Garden of Eden, and he broke covenant with God by eating from the forbidden tree. As a result, Adam faced several curses. His work would not be easy as it was in paradise. Now he would have to labor "in the sweat" (Gen. 3:19) while his harvest would yield "thorns and thistles" (Gen. 3:18). Even the ground on which he worked would be cursed (Gen. 3:17). The ultimate curse, however, was death, when Adam would return to the ground at the end of his life: "for out of it you were taken; you are dust, and to dust you shall return" (Gen. 3:19).

In his Passion and death, Jesus entered into the trial of Adam and took on Adam's curses which had plagued humanity since the time of the Fall. Just like Adam, Jesus was *tested in a garden*—the Garden of Gethsemane—the night before he died (Mt. 26:36–46). There, he took on Adam's *sweat*, as Luke's Gospel points out: Christ's "sweat became like great drops of blood" falling from his face (Lk. 22:44). And he took on Adam's *thorns* as the Roman soldiers mockingly placed a crown of thorns upon his head (Mt. 27:29). Finally, Jesus even entered into Adam's *death* by going to "*a tree*" (Gal. 3:13)—the wood of the Cross—and dying on Calvary. And like Adam, Jesus went down to *the ground* where he was buried—and it was precisely by meeting humanity at that despairingly darkest point that he could lift Adam and the human race out of the grave with him in his victory over all sin and death on Easter morning (Mt. 27:59–61; 28:1–10).[2] As the New Adam, Jesus has redeemed not just Israel, but the entire human race (Rom. 5:12–21).

FAITH OF OUR FATHERS

Let us consider one final Old Testament prefiguring which sheds much light on the mystery of the Cross: Jesus' sacrifice as the fulfillment of what God swore he would do for the patriarch Abraham, the great father of faith for the people of Israel.

In the later years of Abraham's life, God put his faith to a most severe test. He told Abraham, "Take your son, your only-begotten son Isaac, whom you love, and go to the land of Moriah, and offer him there as a burnt offering upon one of the mountains of which I shall tell you" (Gen. 22:2). Abraham rose early the next morning, cut the wood for the offering, saddled his donkey, and traveled with his son to Moriah just as God had instructed. When they arrived, they ascended the mountain with Isaac carrying the wood for the sacrifice on his shoulders. After reaching the top, Abraham prepared the altar for the sacrifice and then bound his son and placed him on the wood. The sacrifice was ready to begin.

> Then Abraham put forth his hand, and took the knife to slay his son. But the angel of the LORD

---

[2] On the Adam-Christ parallels, see Scott Hahn, *A Father Who Keeps His Promises* (Ann Arbor: Servant Publications, 1998), 63–76.

called to him from heaven, and said, "Abraham, Abraham! . . . Do not lay your hand on the lad or do anything to him; for now I know that you fear God, seeing you have not withheld your son, your only son, from me." (Gen. 22:10–12)

The story ends with God rewarding Abraham with a most amazing promise. Because Abraham was willing to give God everything, God swore a covenant oath that he would use Abraham's family as the instrument to bless to the entire world. Through Abraham's descendants, all the nations would find God's blessing.

By myself I have sworn . . . because you have done this, and have not withheld your son, your only son, I will indeed bless you, and I will multiply your descendants . . . and by your descendants shall all the nations of the earth bless themselves, because you have obeyed my voice. (Gen. 22:16–18)

Most commentators on this passage discuss the great faith of Abraham. Few, however, ponder the incredible faith *Isaac* must have had. Imagine what Isaac was feeling when he saw his own dad tie him up, put him on the altar, and bring out a knife to slay him!

But let's look at this story more closely. Even before, when Abraham had completed the ritual procedures for building and preparing the altar for sacrifice, there would have been plenty of time for Isaac to realize that he was the one to be sacrificed. He even might have had time to run away.[3] Also, the Bible reveals that Isaac was old and strong enough to carry the wood for the sacrifice up the mountain and mature enough to understand the intricacies of sacrificial rituals (Gen 22:7–8). Isaac, at the time, certainly was not a tiny child, and he probably was old enough to resist his elderly father, who was over one hundred years old at the time. This is why

Jesus entered into the trial of Adam and took on Adam's curses.

many ancient Jewish rabbis and early Christians saw that Isaac was a voluntary victim who willingly submitted to being offered in obedience to God's command. They assumed Isaac was not a little boy but someone already coming of age, and that Isaac freely chose to go along with God's plan, even if it meant his own death.[4] Now *that's* faith!

This suspenseful story about Abraham and Isaac, however, is much more than a tale of tremendous trust in the Lord. It is also a prophetic sign pointing to how God eventually would accomplish his saving plan for all humanity. Let's look a little closer at this story, and we will see how the offering of Isaac on Moriah prefigures what will actually happen to Jesus at the same

---

[3] G. Wenham, *Genesis 16–50* (Waco: Word, 1987), 114–15: "The Old Testament nowhere speaks of sacrificial animals having their legs bound before slaughter, and if Isaac had been reluctant to be sacrificed, it would have been easier for Abraham to have cut his throat or stabbed him rather than tie him up first and then place him on the altar. But he was tied, indicating his own willing submission to God's command revealed to his father." See also Scott Hahn, *Kinship by Covenant* (Ann Arbor: UMI Dissertation Services, 1995), 194–95.

[4] Wenham, *Genesis 16–50*; Hahn, *Kinship by Covenant*.

place some two thousand years later.

Mount Moriah wasn't any ordinary mountain. It was the sacred place which later came to be known as Jerusalem (cf. 2 Chron. 3:1; Ps. 76:1–3). With this background, we can see some profound parallels between the sacrifice of Isaac and the sacrifice of Jesus on the Cross. Both Isaac and Jesus are described as *beloved sons* (Gen 22:2; Mark 1:11). Just as Abraham offered his beloved son, Isaac, on Mount *Moriah*—which later became associated with Jerusalem—so did our heavenly Father offer his only *beloved Son* on Calvary, just outside *Jerusalem*. Like Isaac, who journeyed to Mount Moriah with a *donkey*, Jesus traveled up that same mountain in a similar way, entering Jerusalem on a *donkey*. Just as Isaac carried the *sacrificial wood* up the mountain, so Jesus shouldered the *wood for the sacrifice*—the wood of the Cross—to Calvary.

And when Jesus arrived at Calvary broken, beaten, and barely walking, he willingly stretched out his hands and laid his body on the wood, allowing himself to be nailed to the Cross and offering himself as a *voluntary sacrifice*—reminiscent of Isaac's *free sacrificial offering of himself* on that same mountain.

This time, however, there was no angel to stop the sacrifice, for the Son was determined to offer himself like a lamb on our behalf. And he did all this in order to bring about the worldwide blessing which God—right there on Moriah—swore he would carry out through Abraham's children. Indeed, Jesus was that faithful "son of Abraham" (Mt. 1:1), that faithful Israelite, through whom a broken human family would find healing and reunion with its heavenly Father.

Israel's mission to the nations was finally accomplished. Through Jesus, God's blessing went out from Israel to embrace the whole world. Through Israel's royal representative—Jesus—God's people finally became what they were always meant to be: light to the world.

And Israel's light never shined brighter than when it pierced the tomb on Easter morning and overpowered the darkness which covered the face of the earth.

QUESTIONS FOR DISCUSSION

1. What are some of the ways Matthew's Gospel shows us Christ' crucifixion is not his moment of defeat, but his triumph as Israel's king?

2. What scene from Christ's Passion and death moves your heart the most? Why?

3. In Matthew 26:17–29, we see Jesus is the new Passover Lamb. How does Jesus associate himself with the Passover lamb at the Last Supper? How does this Passover background shed light on Jesus' sacrifice on the Cross on Good Friday?

4. In Christ's Passion, Jesus takes on the curses of Adam. Read Genesis 3:17–19. What are the various punishments given to Adam for his sin in these verses? How does Jesus take on these punishments of Adam in his Passion and death?

5. In what ways does the sacrifice of Isaac in the Old Testament prefigure Christ's being offered in sacrifice on Calvary (See Genesis 22:1–18)?

Chapter 14

Great Commission

All authority in heaven and on earth has been
given to me. Go therefore and make disciples of
all nations, baptizing them in the name of the
Father and of the Son and of the Holy Spirit,
teaching them to observe all that I have commanded you; and lo, I am with you always, to
the close of the age. (Mt. 28:18–20)

THESE WORDS represent the first—and last—words Jesus
speaks to his apostles after his Resurrection in Matthew's Gospel. Other Gospels include various accounts
of the risen Jesus first appearing to the apostles—at
a table (Mk. 16:14), in Jerusalem (Lk. 24:33–36), in a
room with the doors shut (Jn. 20:19, 26). Matthew tells
of a time Jesus appeared to the apostles on a mountain

in Galilee, thus bringing the story full circle to where Jesus first called his disciples (Mt. 4:18–22) and the region where he gave his great "sermon on the mount" (Mt. 5:1). Now, on a mountain in Galilee once more, Jesus gathers his apostles together for one final great commissioning—words that tie together two important themes in Matthew's Gospel: Jesus' *authority as the Messiah* and *his presence with his people.*

First, Jesus' authority: Throughout the Gospel, Matthew has been preparing his readers for understanding Jesus' full authority as the Messiah-King. We saw how in the opening chapter, Jesus is introduced in the genealogy with kingly authority, coming as the climactic Son of David in a long line of Davidic heirs. At the start of his messianic mission, Jesus' authority is seen when he is anointed with the Spirit at his baptism (Mt. 3:16–17) and as he withstands Satan's three temptations in the desert. Throughout his ministry, Jesus' authority is exhibited in his powerful teaching ("he taught them as one with authority, not as the scribes") (Mt. 7:28–29), and in his powerful actions of calming storms, healing the sick, forgiving sins, and exorcising demons—demonstrating his authority over all creation, all physical ailments, sin, and even evil spirits (cf. Mt. 9:33). All this, however, was but a prelude to the ultimate manifestation of Jesus' supreme authority which came in his death and Resurrection. Only now, after defeating sin and death in his rising from the dead, does Jesus make this triumphant declaration to his apostles: "All authority in heaven and on earth has been given to me."

Here, Daniel's image of the "Son of man" will come in handy again. Recall how in Daniel's vision the Son of man figure represented God's people as they were trampled over by the four great kingdoms symbolized by the four fierce beasts (cf. Dan. 7:23–27). But then, rather surprisingly, the Son of man was rescued by God and is given *authority* to rule over all the earth.

Like the mysterious figure in Daniel, Jesus also shared the suffering of God's people. There on the Cross, Jesus experienced firsthand the beasts swarming around him in full force, as the enemies of God's people persecuted him and brought him to his death.

But this wasn't the end of the story. Just as God delivered the Son of man in Daniel 7 from the evil powers, so did God rescue Jesus in his darkest hour, raising him from the tomb on Easter morning. Only now, as the Son of man vindicated and victorious, does Jesus proclaim his dominion over all things, saying to the apostles: "All authority in heaven and on earth has been given to me." Jesus brings the story of Daniel 7 to its fulfillment in his Resurrection.

Now it is up to the apostles to continue Christ's mission by bringing his kingdom to the whole world. This is why Jesus commissions the apostles to go out to all the earth teaching and baptizing all peoples:

> Go therefore and make disciples of all nations, baptizing them in the name of the Father and of the Son and of the Holy Spirit, teaching them to observe all that I have commanded you. (Mt. 28:19–20)

Recall how in Matthew 10 Jesus already bestowed upon the apostles his very authority to announce the kingdom in his name by preaching and healing just as he had done (Mt. 10:1–15). In that first commissioning, however, Jesus sent them out only to "the lost sheep of the house of Israel" (Mt. 10:6). But now, after the Resurrection, Christ's kingdom bursts out across all borders. Now that the Messiah-King has freed God's people from their true oppressors, light can finally pour forth from Israel to all the nations. Jesus will finally accomplish what Israel was always meant to do: bring all peoples back into union with the one true God. And he will do that through his apostles. Invested with the authority of the Messiah-King himself, the apostles are commissioned to gather all nations into Christ's kingdom and carry out his triumph over sin and death in the lives of people all over the world.

Matthew's Gospel ends in the same place it began: with the theme of Emmanuel.

STILL EMMANUEL

They won't be alone in that mission. Jesus promises to *be with* the apostles until the end of time. And this takes us to our second theme in the Great Commission—the theme of Emmanuel, of God being *with* his disciples. Here, Matthew's Gospel ends in the same place it began. We saw how the first chapter of the Gospel culminated with Jesus' receiving the glorious title "Emmanuel," meaning *God with us* (Mt. 1:23). Now, twenty-seven chapters later, at the close of the Gospel, Emmanuel himself promises to "*be with*" the apostles in their mission of bringing the kingdom to all the nations.

And like the apostles, we won't be alone in our mission. The same Jesus who promised to be with the apostles two thousand years ago continues to be with us as we help build Christ's kingdom in the world today. He promises to be with us when we pray, especially whenever two or three are gathered in his name (Mt. 18:20). He is with us in the inspired words of Scripture, through which God speaks lovingly to us as his children (cf. CCC 80, 104). He is with us in the Church through the bishops, who serve as the apostles' successors and Christ's representatives in their shepherding and teaching of the Christian people (cf. CCC 860). He is with us in a special way in the poor (Mt. 25: 31–46). And most intimately, Jesus remains with us in his Real Presence in the Holy Eucharist, which fills us with his very life during our journey here on earth (cf. CCC 1373–81). Confident in Jesus' presence with us, we are now called to go forward and bring the kingdom of Christ to a broken, wounded world that is longing for the healing, freedom, and love that only Christ can give.

QUESTIONS FOR DISCUSSION

1. Jesus commissions the apostles to go make disciples of all nations. What can you do to live this mission of evangelization more today?

2. In his last words in the Gospel of Matthew, Jesus promises to be with us even to the end of the age. What are some of the many ways Jesus remains with us today as Catholics? Which way has been a particular source of encouragement and help to you? Which way do you think you need to seek out more?

3. Looking back over the many themes and scenes we've explored in Matthew's Gospel, which insight do you appreciate most? Why?

About the Author

DR. EDWARD SRI is a theologian, author, and well-known Catholic speaker who appears regularly on EWTN. Each year he speaks to clergy, parish leaders, catechists, and laity from around the world.

He has written several Catholic best-selling books, including *No Greater Love: A Biblical Walk through Christ's Passion* (Ascension); *Men, Women and the Mystery of Love* (Servant); *A Biblical Walk Through the Mass* (Ascension); *Walking with Mary* (Image); and *Who Am I to Judge?: Responding to Relativism with Logic and Love* (Ignatius Press).

He also is the coauthor with Curtis Mitch of a more extensive commentary on Matthew's Gospel in the Catholic Commentary on Sacred Scripture Series called *The Gospel of Matthew* (Baker Academic).

Edward Sri is the presenter of several popular faith formation programs, including *Mary: A Biblical Walk with the Blessed Mother* (Ascension) and *No Greater Love: A Biblical Walk through Christ's Passion* (Ascension). He is also the host of the film series *Symbolon:*

The Catholic Faith Explained (Augustine Institute).

He is a founding leader with Curtis Martin of FOCUS (Fellowship of Catholic University Students) and currently serves as FOCUS vice president of formation.

Dr. Sri is also the host of the weekly podcast *All Things Catholic* and leads pilgrimages to Rome and the Holy Land each year. He holds a doctorate from the Pontifical University of St. Thomas Aquinas in Rome and is an adjunct professor at the Augustine Institute. He resides with his wife Elizabeth and their eight children in Littleton, Colorado.

You can connect with Edward Sri through his website EdwardSri.com or follow him on Facebook, Twitter, and Instagram.